# QURAN, HADITH, AND ISLAM

by

Rashad Khalifa, Ph.D.

Published by Universal Unity
1860 Mowry Ave. Suite 400
Fremont, CA 94538
Fax: (510) 794-9783
Web site: http://www.universalunity.net
e-mail: books@universalunity.net

In collaboration with United Submitters International
Masjid Tucson
PO Box 43476
Tucson, AZ 85733-3476
Tel/Fax (520)323-7636
Web site: http://www.masjidtucson.org

Manufactured in the United States of America

10   9   8   7   6   5   4

Library of Congress Cataloging-in Publication Data

Khalifa, Rashad
   QURAN, HADITH, AND ISLAM / by Dr. Rashad Khalifa
   p. cm.
   English and Arabic
   ISBN 1881893-04-9 (alk. paper)
   1. Islam—Controversial literature. 2. Koran—Controversial literature.
   3.    Hadith—Controversial literature. I. Title.

   BP169  K45 2000
   297.1'2-dc21                                                      00-051227

# PREFACE

## TO THIS EDITION

On January 31, 1990, sometime before dawn, Dr. Rashad Khalifa was martyred by one or more disbelievers who broke into the masjid earlier that night and waited for him to come in. It was a well known fact that Dr. Khalifa would come every day in the early hours to carry on his work on the Quran translation.

Dr. Rashad Khalifa was the author of several books. This book is being printed for the first time after his death. Nothing has been deleted or added.

Universal Unity
Fremont, December 21st, 2000

# PREFACE

(FIRST PRINTING)

After more than 12 years of computerized research of Quran, PHYSICAL EVIDENCE was discovered proving that Quran is indeed the infallible word of God. This discovery became very popular among the Muslim masses throughout the world, and summaries of the work were printed and distributed by the millions. My personal popularity soared along with this most exciting, and most humbling, discovery.

The continued research then unveiled a startling fact; that the extremely popular "Hadith & Sunna" have nothing to do with the prophet Muhammad, and that adherence thereto represents flagrant disobedience of God and His final prophet (Quran 6:112 & 25:31). This finding contradicts the beliefs of Muslim masses everywhere. Consequently, my personal popularity, and even the popularity of the Quran's miracle, plunged to the point of endangering my life and reputation. As it turned out telling the Muslims that "Hadith & Sunna" are Satanic inventions is the same as telling the Christians that Jesus is not the son of God.

Since the recognition of "Hadith & Sunna" as Satanic innovations is supported by PHYSICAL EVIDENCE, all free thinking people will accept the findings reported in this book. For such people, the results include a totally new sense of salvation, and full awareness that the Muslim masses have fallen victim to Satan's schemes.

Rashad Khalifa

August 19, 1982

## NO SALVATION WITHOUT OBEYING THE MESSENGER

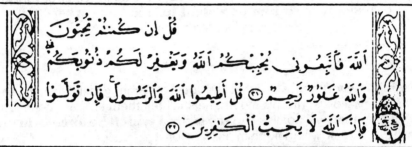

"Say (O Muhammad), 'If you love God, then follow me. God will then love you, and forgive your sins; God is forgiver, merciful.' Say, 'Obey God and the messenger.' If they turn away, then God loves not the disbelievers." (3: 31-32)

---

"You shall observe Salat & Zakat, and obey the messenger, that you may attain mercy."     (24: 56)

---

"Anyone who disobeys God and His messenger will abide in the fire of hell forever."     ( 72: 23 )

- - - - - - - - - - - - - - - - - - - - - - - - - - - - - - - - - - - - - - -

Since all the messengers delivered one and the same message, namely, "YOU SHALL NOT WORSHIP EXCEPT GOD," disobeying them constitutes disbelief, or idol-worship.

---

## WHEN DELIVERING GOD'S MESSAGES,
### messengers do not speak on their own initiative.

---

A prophet like me, will the Lord, your God, raise up for you from among your own kinsmen; **to him you shall listen.**

(Moses in Deuteronomy 18:15)

---

I will raise up for them a prophet like you from among their kinsmen, and will put my words into his mouth; he shall tell them all that I command him. If any man will not listen to **my words which he speaks in my name,** I myself will make him answer for it.

(Deuteronomy 18:18-19)

---

10 "Do you not believe that I am in the Father, and the Father is in me? The words that I say to you **I do not speak on My own initiative, but the Father abiding in Me does His works.**

Gospel of John 14:10

---

13 "But when He, the Spirit of truth, comes, He will guide you into all the truth; for **He will not speak on His own initiative,** but whatever He hears, He will speak; and He will disclose to you what is to come.

John 16:13

---

Obeying the Messenger is obeying God.
(Quran 4:80)

وَمَا يَنطِقُ عَنِ ٱلْهَوَىٰٓ ﴿

---

"and he (Muhammad) does not speak on his own initiative".     (53:3)

## MUHAMMAD REPRESENTED BY QURAN ALONE

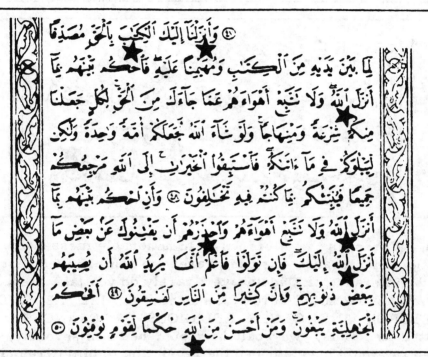

"We sent down to you <u>THIS BOOK</u> truthfully, confirming all previous scriptures, and superseding them. You shall judge among them according to what is sent down from God (this book), and do not follow their wishes if they deviate from the truth. ... You shall judge among them according to what is sent down from God (this book); do not follow their wishes, and BEWARE lest they divert you from that which is sent down to you from God (this book). ... Would they seek the laws of ignorance? <u>WHO IS BETTER THAN GOD</u> as a law-maker, for those who sincerely believe?" (5: 48-50)

## MUHAMMAD FORBIDDEN FROM UTTERING ANY RELIGIOUS INSTRUCTIONS OTHER THAN QURAN

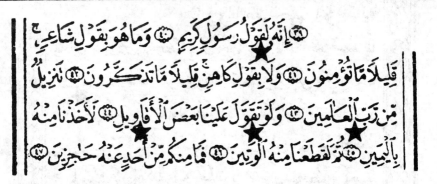

"This (Quran) is the utterance of an honorable messenger. It is not the utterance of a poet; rarely do you believe. Nor is it the utterance of a soothsayer; rarely do you take heed. A revelation from the Lord of the universe. HAD HE EVER UTTERED ANY OTHER RELIGIOUS UTTERANCES (attributed to us), we would have punished him severely, then we would have stopped the revelation to him (fired him). None of you could have protected him against us."(69:40-47)

-------------------------------------------------------------

These very clear verses teach us that Muhammad was forbidden from uttering any religious teachings beside Quran. The strength of the Arabic text cannot be fully translated to English. But the powerful expressions leave no doubt whatsoever that the Prophet's sole function was to "DELIVER" Quran, the whole Quran, and NOTHING but Quran.

---

**MUHAMMAD ORDERED NEVER TO DEVIATE FROM QURAN. DEVIATION MEANT SEVERE PUNISHMENT**

---

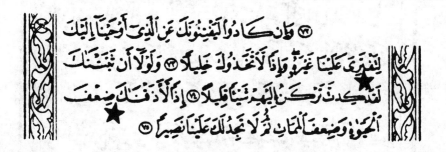

---

"They <u>almost</u> diverted you (O Muhammad) from our revelations to you; they wanted you to fabricate something else to consider you a friend. If it were not that we strengthened you, you <u>almost</u> leaned towards them a little bit. Had you done it, we would have doubled the punishment for you in this life, and after death; no one could have protected you against us. " (17: 73-75)

------------------------------------------------

In setting the example for us, the Prophet was ordered to adhere strictly to God's revelations to Him, specifically identified in 5:48-50 (Page 3) as Quran.

The slightest deviation from Quran (see verse 74 above) incurs severe retribution.

Muhammad ordered to deliver QURAN ALONE, without the least alteration, and never to "fabricate" anything else:

سورة يونس ⑭ وَإِذَا تُتْلَى عَلَيْهِمْ ءَايَاتُنَا بَيِّنَاتٍ قَالَ الَّذِينَ
لَا يَرْجُونَ لِقَآءَنَا ائْتِ بِقُرْآنٍ غَيْرِ هَذَا أَوْ بَدِّلْهُ قُلْ مَا يَكُونُ لِي
أَنْ أُبَدِّلَهُ مِن تِلْقَآئِ نَفْسِي إِنْ أَتَّبِعُ إِلَّا مَا يُوحَى إِلَيَّ إِنِّي أَخَافُ إِنْ
عَصَيْتُ رَبِّي عَذَابَ يَوْمٍ عَظِيمٍ ⑮ قُلْ لَوْ شَآءَ اللَّهُ مَا تَلَوْتُهُ عَلَيْكُمْ
وَلَا أَدْرَاكُم بِهِ فَقَدْ لَبِثْتُ فِيكُمْ عُمُرًا مِّن قَبْلِهِ أَفَلَا تَعْقِلُونَ ⑯
فَمَنْ أَظْلَمُ مِمَّنِ افْتَرَى عَلَى اللَّهِ كَذِبًا أَوْ كَذَّبَ بِآيَاتِهِ إِنَّهُ لَا يُفْلِحُ
الْمُجْرِمُونَ ⑰ وَيَعْبُدُونَ مِن دُونِ اللَّهِ مَا لَا يَضُرُّهُمْ وَلَا يَنفَعُهُمْ
وَيَقُولُونَ هَؤُلَاءِ شُفَعَاؤُنَا عِندَ اللَّهِ قُلْ أَتُنَبِّئُونَ اللَّهَ بِمَا لَا يَعْلَمُ
فِي السَّمَاوَاتِ وَلَا فِي الْأَرْضِ سُبْحَانَهُ وَتَعَالَى عَمَّا يُشْرِكُونَ ⑱

"When our verses are recited for them, those who do not expect to meet us would say, 'Bring a Quran other than this or change it.' Say (O Muhammad), 'I cannot change it on m own initiative. I simply follow what is revealed to me. I fear, if I disobey my Lord, the retribution of a terrible day ...Who is more wicked than one who invents lies about God or rejects His revelations? The guilty never succeed. Yet, they idolize beside God those who possess no power to harn them or benefit them, and say, 'These are our intercessors with God.' ...such is idol-worship." (10: 15-18)

```
ONE  GOD  /  ONE  SOURCE
```

   Our Almighty Creator commands that QURAN, specifically QURAN, SHALL BE THE ONLY SOURCE of
religious teachings.

   Furthermore, we are told that THE ACCEPTANCE
OF ANY OTHER SOURCES for religious guidance equals
the setting up of OTHER GODS BESIDE GOD:

"Say (O Muhammad), 'Whose testimony is greater?' Say,
'God is the witness between me and you that THIS QURAN
was given to me to preach it to you, and to whomever it
reaches.' However, you certainly bear witness that you
set up other gods beside God (by upholding other sources
beside Quran). Say, 'I will never do what you are doing;
I disown your idol-worship.'"        ( 6: 19 )

- - - - - - - - - - - - - - - - - - - - - - - - - - - - - - -

This profound verse, which happens to be verse [ 19 ] of
Sura 6, enjoins the believers from upholding or following
ANY OTHER SOURCE BESIDE QURAN, and that doing
this is equivalent to the setting up of other gods beside God.

---

# ONE GOD / ONE SOURCE

---

In the strictest possible language, we are commanded to uphold Quran, the whole Quran, and nothing but Quran.

Repeatedly, we are commanded to uphold Quran as the ONLY SOURCE OF RELIGIOUS GUIDANCE.

Again and again, we are reminded that the following of ANY OTHER SOURCE BESIDE QURAN EQUALS THE SETTING UP OF OTHER GODS BESIDE GOD.

------------------------------------------------------------

Verses 22 through 38 of Sura 17 represent some of the most important commandments in Quran. Immediately following these verses we find the verse shown below:

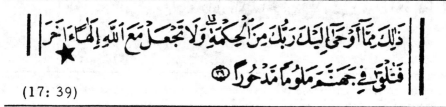

(17: 39)

"This is some of the wisdom revealed to you (in this Quran), and YOU SHALL NOT SET UP ANY OTHER GOD BE-SIDE GOD (by following any other source beside Quran). Otherwise, you will be thrown into hell, blamed and debased.

------------------------------------------------------------

Despite all these clear commandments and extremely strict injunctions, why do the followers of Hadith & Sunna fail to uphold the Quran alone? See the answer on Page 9.

## QURAN: AN EXTRAORDINARY BOOK

Despite the clear commandments, why do the followers of <u>Hadith & Sunna</u> fail to uphold Quran ALONE ?

The answer is provided in the same Sura following the commandment shown on Page 8. Verses 45 and 46 of Sura 17 inform us that those who refuse to believe God and heed His commandment to uphold Quran <u>ALONE</u> are deliberately isolated from Quran. These two crucial verses are shown below:

---

وَإِذَا قَرَأْتَ ٱلْقُرْءَانَ جَعَلْنَا ۝ بَيْنَكَ وَبَيْنَ ٱلَّذِينَ لَا يُؤْمِنُونَ بِٱلْأَخِرَةِ حِجَابًا مَّسْتُورًا ۝ وَجَعَلْنَا عَلَىٰ قُلُوبِهِمْ أَكِنَّةً أَن يَفْقَهُوهُ وَفِىٓ ءَاذَانِهِمْ وَقْرًا وَإِذَا ذَكَرْتَ رَبَّكَ فِى ٱلْقُرْءَانِ وَحْدَهُۥ وَلَّوْاْ عَلَىٰٓ أَدْبَٰرِهِمْ نُفُورًا ۝

---

"When you read the Quran, we place between you and those who do not believe in the Hereafter an invisible barrier. And we place shields on their hearts, to prevent them from understanding Quran, and deafness in their ears. Consequently, when you preach your Lord <u>IN THE QURAN ALONE</u> they run away in aversion." (17:45-46)

------------------------------------------------

WHAT MORE CAN WE SAY ??

## DO YOU BELIEVE GOD OR NOT ?

God says that Quran is <u>COMPLETE, PERFECT, & FULLY DETAILED</u>, and that you shall not seek any other source:

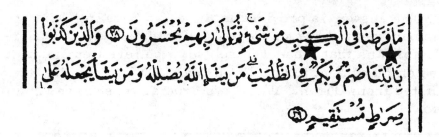

"We did not leave anything out of this book, then all will be gathered before their Lord (for judgment). Those who do not believe our verses are deaf and dumb; in total darkness. God sends astray whomever He wills, and directs whomever He wills in the right path." (6: 38-39)

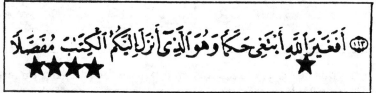

"Shall I seek other than God as a source of law, when He revealed <u>THIS BOOK FULLY DETAILED</u>? (6: 114)

(6: 115) وَتَمَّتْ كَلِمَتُ رَبِّكَ صِدْقًا وَعَدْلًا

"The word of your Lord is <u>COMPLETE</u> in truth & justice"

## THE CONSEQUENCE OF NOT BELIEVING GOD

As shown on Page 10, God says that Quran is COMPLETE, PERFECT, AND FULLY DETAILED.

His commandments are clear and strict that YOU SHALL NOT UPHOLD ANYTHING ELSE BESIDE QURAN as a source of religious guidance (see pages 7 & 8).

Now, you have the total freedom to decide to believe God, or to reject His statements, and ignore His commandments, provided you are willing (or unwilling) to accept the consequences.

You agree, no doubt, that refusing to believe God is a very serious offense. Just how serious is expressed in verse 40 of Sura 7:

( 7: 40 )

وَإِنَّ الَّذِينَ كَذَّبُوا۟ بِـَٔايَـٰتِنَا وَٱسْتَكْبَرُوا۟ عَنْهَا لَا تُفَتَّحُ لَهُمْ أَبْوَٰبُ ٱلسَّمَآءِ وَلَا يَدْخُلُونَ ٱلْجَنَّةَ حَتَّىٰ يَلِجَ ٱلْجَمَلُ فِى سَمِّ ٱلْخِيَاطِ وَكَذَٰلِكَ نَجْزِى ٱلْمُجْرِمِينَ

"Surely, those who do not believe our revelations, and are too arrogant to heed them, the gates of the sky never open for them, nor will they ever enter Paradise until the camel passes through the needle's eye. We thus requite the guilty."

-------------------------------------------------------------

Thus, it is A PHYSICAL IMPOSSIBILITY for those who refuse to believe God to enter Paradise.

## IMPORTANT CRITERION OF DIVINE REVELATION

Some people claim that the "Hadith & Sunna" are divine revelations. Obviously, they are not aware that the criterion of
divine revelation is PERFECT PRESERVATION. Since the
so-called hadith & sunna of the Prophet have been vastly
corrupted, they can never meet the criterion of divine revelation. It is an acknowledged fact that the vast majority of
Hadiths are false fabrications.

---

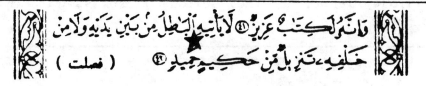

"We have sent down the revelation, and we will surely pre-
serve it." (15: 9)

---

"Indeed, this is an honorable scripture. Falsehood could
never enter it in the past, present, or future; a revelation
from the most wise, the most praised." (41: 41-42)

- - - - - - - - - - - - - - - - - - - - - - - - - - - - - - - - - - - - - - - - -

The blasphemy is evident when they claim that Hadith
and Sunna are divine revelations. Do they not realize that
God Almighty is capable of preserving His revelations?

## HADITH & SUNNA = 100% CONJECTURE

Although God declares that Quran is FULLY DETAILED, & shall be the only source, the majority of Muslims have been duped into following the conjecture known as Hadith & Sunna.

While Quran is proven by PHYSICAL EVIDENCE to be the authentic and unaltered word of God (see the book, "QURAN: VISUAL PRESENTATION OF THE MIRACLE"), Hadith and Sunna are unanimously recognized as conjecture.

( 6: 114-116)

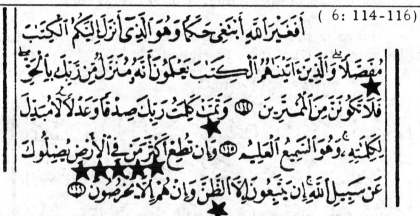

"Shall I seek OTHER THAN GOD as a source of law, when He has revealed THIS BOOK FULLY DETAILED? .....
The word of your Lord is COMPLETE, in truth and justice. Nothing shall abrogate His words; He is the hearer, the omniscient. Yet, if you obey the majority of people, they will take you away from the path of God. That is because they follow CONJECTURE, and they fail to think."

"They insist upon following conjecture, when the guidance is given to them herein from their Lord." ( 53: 23 )

## OBEYING THE MESSENGER IS CONDITIONED

Obeying the messenger is absolute only as far as the Quranic revelations are concerned.

Obeying the messenger is in upholding Quran, the whole Quran, and nothing but Quran.

Obedience is strictly ON CONDITION THAT the source is God through the messenger, and not the messenger who is no more than a human being, subject to errors.

As shown in the verse below, the messenger as a man is to be obeyed ONLY if he is right:

(60: 12)

يَـٰٓأَيُّهَا ٱلنَّبِيُّ إِذَا جَآءَكَ ٱلۡمُؤۡمِنَـٰتُ

يُبَايِعۡنَكَ عَلَىٰٓ أَن لَّا يُشۡرِكۡنَ بِٱللَّهِ شَيۡـًٔا وَلَا يَسۡرِقۡنَ وَلَا يَزۡنِينَ وَلَا

يَقۡتُلۡنَ أَوۡلَـٰدَهُنَّ وَلَا يَأۡتِينَ بِبُهۡتَـٰنٍ يَفۡتَرِينَهُۥ بَيۡنَ أَيۡدِيهِنَّ

وَأَرۡجُلِهِنَّ وَلَا يَعۡصِينَكَ فِي مَعۡرُوفٍ فَبَايِعۡهُنَّ وَٱسۡتَغۡفِرۡ لَهُنَّ ٱللَّهَ

★ ★ ★

"O prophet, if the believing women come to you and pledge that they will not idolize anything beside God, nor steal, nor commit adultery, nor kill their children, nor produce any falsehood, nor disobey you WHEN YOU ARE RIGHT, you shall accept their pledge, and ask God to forgive them."

- - - - - - - - - - - - - - - - - - - - - - - - - - - - - - - - - - - - -

Thus, the condition is evident that Muhammad the man, unlike Muhammad the messenger, shall be obeyed ONLY IF HE IS RIGHT.

## OBEYING THE MESSENGER IS <u>CONDITIONED</u>

The Quran emphasizes that obedience is absolute when the source is God, while the personal opinion of the messenger may be detrimental to him and/or to those who follow his personal opinions:

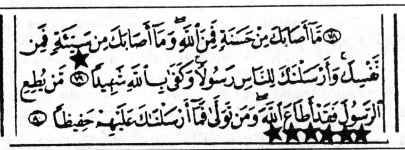

"Anything good that happens to you (O Muhammad) is from God. And anything bad that happens to you is <u>from you</u>. We have sent you as a messenger to the people, and God suffices as a witness. Whoever obeys the messenger is obeying God. As for those who turn away, we did not send you as their guardian." (4: 79-80)

- - - - - - - - - - - - - - - - - - - - - - - - - - - - - - - - - - - -

Thus, the personal opinion of Muhammad may be bad, and may cause bad things to happen. On the other hand, Muhammad the messenger utters THE WORDS OF GOD, i.e., the Quran, and must be obeyed absolutely. For whoever obeys the messenger is obeying God, and we are to obey the commandments of God, not the commandments of men.

## OBEYING THE MESSENGER IS CONDITIONED

The Quran gives numerous examples that we must obey what Muhammad uttered as a messenger of God, and NOT NECESSARILY what he uttered as a man. As a messenger, he uttered Quran, and nothing but Quran.

Furthermore, the Quran teaches that Muhammad the man actually committed serious errors. Thus, in the verse shown below we see that God wished to establish a law whereby a man can marry the divorced wife of his adopted son. Muhammad was to be our example. However, this was contrary to the traditions of Arabia, and the Prophet actually "feared the people instead of fearing God."

وَإِذْ تَقُولُ لِلَّذِى أَنْعَمَ اللَّهُ عَلَيْهِ وَأَنْعَمْتَ عَلَيْهِ أَمْسِكْ عَلَيْكَ زَوْجَكَ وَاتَّقِ اللَّهَ وَتُخْفِى فِى نَفْسِكَ مَا اللَّهُ مُبْدِيهِ وَتَخْشَى النَّاسَ وَاللَّهُ أَحَقُّ أَنْ تَخْشَاهُ فَلَمَّا قَضَى زَيْدٌ مِنْهَا وَطَرًا زَوَّجْنَاكَهَا لِكَىْ لَا يَكُونَ عَلَى الْمُؤْمِنِينَ حَرَجٌ فِى أَزْوَاجِ أَدْعِيَائِهِمْ إِذَا قَضَوْا مِنْهُنَّ وَطَرًا وَكَانَ أَمْرُ اللَّهِ مَفْعُولًا ۝

(33: 37)

"You said to the one blessed by God and blessed by you, 'Do not divorce your wife, and observe God.' Thus, you hid in yourself what God wanted to declare, and you feared the people when God is the one you should fear. Then, when Zeid (Muhammad's adopted son) finally divorced her, we had you marry her. This was done to show that the believing men are allowed to marry the divorced wives of their adopted sons. The commands of God shall be carried out."

## OBEYING THE MESSENGER IS <u>CONDITIONED</u>

One complete Sura illustrates the fact that we are to obey Muhammad ONLY in his Quranic utterances, and NOT in his personal utterances or personal behavior. This rules out the so-called "<u>Hadith</u>" and the so-called "<u>Sunna</u>' as legitimate sources of religious guidance.

The Sura is entitled " 'Abasa = He Frowned", and narrates an incident where Muhammad ignored a poor blind man, and gave his full attention to a rich man:

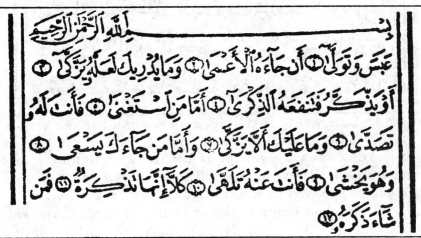

"He (Muhammad) frowned and turned away, when the blind man came to him. How do you know; he may be saved? Or, he may heed the message and benefit by such heeding. As for the rich man, you (Muhammad) gave him your attention. Even though you cannot guarantee his salvation. But the one who came to you seeking salvation, and sincerely reverent, you disregarded him. Indeed, THIS IS A REMINDER, for those who choose to remember. (80: 1-12)

---

## THE IDOLIZATION OF MUHAMMAD

---

Refusing to believe God in His repeated assertions that the QURAN IS COMPLETE, PERFECT, & SHALL BE THE ONLY SOURCE of religious guidance, and following the conjecture known as <u>Hadith & Sunna</u> constitutes deification of the prophet Muhammad against his will.

---

بِسْمِ اللّٰهِ الرَّحْمٰنِ الرَّحِيمِ

"Say (O Muhammad), 'If the ocean were ink for the words of my Lord, the ocean would have run out before my Lord runs out of words, even if we supplied twice as much ink.' Say (O Muhammad), 'I am no more than a human being like you. It has been revealed to me that your God is ONE GOD. Thus, anyone who looks forward to meeting his Lord shall lead a righteous life, and NEVER SET UP ANY IDOLS beside his Lord.'" (18: 109-110)

------------------------------------------------

These verses clearly inform us that God does not suffer from shortage of words; that He gave us <u>ALL THE WORDS</u> we need in this Quran, and that we should not seek the words of Muhammad, or anyone else, and that Muhammad is a man like other men; he should not be idolized (see end of verse).

---

QURAN: YOU SHALL NOT IDOLIZE MUHAMMAD

---

There are only two verses in Quran that describe the prophet Muhammad as "no more than a human being like you."

IS IT COINCIDENCE THAT <u>BOTH VERSES</u> FORBID

IDOLATRY AT THE END OF EACH VERSE ??

The first verse is shown on the previous page, and the second verse is shown below:

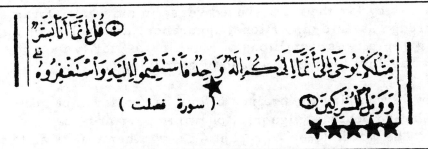

"Say (O Muhammad), 'I am no more than a human being like you. It has been revealed to me that your God is ONE GOD. Therefore, you shall observe Him ALONE, ask His forgiveness, AND <u>WOE TO THE IDOL-WORSHIPERS.</u>'" (41:6)

------------------------------------------------

The true believers believe their Lord in His statements that QURAN IS COMPLETE, PERFECT, FULLY DETAILED, AND SHALL BE THE SOLE SOURCE OF RELIGIOUS GUIDANCE. Only the idol-worshipers will seek other than Quran. Following "Hadith & Sunna" is idolization of the prophet Muhammad against his will.

## THE   ABUSE   OF   QURAN

$$\text{بِسْمِ اللَّهِ وَمَلَائِكَتَهُ يُصَلُّونَ عَلَى النَّبِيِّ يَا أَيُّهَا}$$

$$\text{الَّذِينَ آمَنُوا صَلُّوا عَلَيْهِ وَسَلِّمُوا تَسْلِيمًا}$$

"God and His angels encourage the prophet. O you who believe, you too shall encourage him, and support him completely."(33: 56)

- - - - - - - - - - - - - - - - - - - - - - - - - - - - - - - - - - - - - - -

This is by far the most abused verse in the whole Quran. Through satanic distortions, ignorance, and idol-worship, this verse causes millions of Muslims to glorify the prophet against his will, instead of glorifying God.

People who sing the praises of this particular verse day and night are obviously ignorant of two important facts:

(1)  The word "Naby = prophet = نبى " when referring to the prophet Muhammad <u>ALWAYS</u> refers to him when he was alive; not after his death.

(2)  In the same Sura, and 13 verses <u>ahead</u> of this verse, we find that God and His angels do the same honoring for <u>ALL  THE  BELIEVERS</u>.

$$\text{هُوَ الَّذِي يُصَلِّي عَلَيْكُمْ وَمَلَائِكَتُهُ لِيُخْرِجَكُمْ مِنَ الظُّلُمَاتِ إِلَى النُّورِ}$$

"God and His angels encourage the believers, to take them out of darkness into the light."   (33: 43)

## THE   ABUSE   OF   QURAN

Verse 103 of Sura 9 further clarifies the meaning of the words "SSALLOO" and "YUSSALLEE." In this verse, we see that the Prophet is commanded to "YUSSALLEE" for the believers, just as they are asked to do for him in verse 56 of Sura 33 (see Page 20).

خُذْ مِنْ أَمْوَالِهِمْ صَدَقَةً تُطَهِّرُهُمْ وَتُزَكِّيهِم بِهَا وَصَلِّ عَلَيْهِمْ إِنَّ صَلَوٰتَكَ سَكَنٌ لَّهُمْ وَاللَّهُ سَمِيعٌ عَلِيمٌ ۞

(9: 103)

"Take (O Muhammad) a portion of their money for charity, in order to purify them and sanctify them, and encourage them (SSALLEE 'ALAYHIM) for your encouragement is a consolation for them. God is hearer, omniscient."(9: 103).

Thus, the true meaning of this expression is "encourage," and NOT "praise day and night" as those who abuse the Quran have indicated.

### SUMMARY

1. God and His angels encourage the believers, to take them out of darkness into the light (33: 43).

2. God and His angels encourage the Prophet during his life to keep him on the right path (33: 56).

3. The believers are asked to support the Prophet during his life (33: 56), and the Prophet does the same for the believers (9: 103).

## THE ABUSE OF QURAN

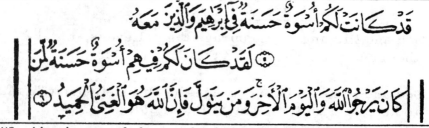

"In the messenger of God, you have a good example; a good example for those who **are** seeking God and the Last day, and commemorate God frequently." (33:21)

---

Satan used this verse to claim a special status for the idolization of Muhammad, and to convince the people of the necessity of <u>Sunna</u> (traditions) of the prophet.

There is no doubt that the prophet Muhammad is our best example. And his example is set by upholding Quran, and nothing but Quran.

Obviously, those who fell in Satan's trap are ignorant of the fact that <u>ABRAHAM IS DESCRIBED IN QURAN IN THE SAME WORDS</u>; word for word.

"In Abraham and those who believed with him, you have a good example; for those who are seeking God and the Last day." (60: 4, 6)

## DOES GOD HATE MUHAMMAD ? ? ?

Of course not.  But when you repeat the same things that
God says about Muhammad in Quran, they accuse you of
hating Muhammad.

Similarly, when you tell the Christians that Jesus is a
human being and a messenger of God, they accuse you of
hating Jesus.

## MUHAMMAD CANNOT GUIDE ANYONE (28: 56)

إِنَّكَ لَا تَهْدِى مَنْ أَحْبَبْتَ وَلَٰكِنَّ ٱللَّهَ يَهْدِى مَن يَشَآءُ وَهُوَ أَعْلَمُ بِٱلْمُهْتَدِينَ ۝ ( سورة القصص )

"You (Muhammad) cannot guide even the ones you love.  God
is the one who guides whomever He wills, for He knows best
those who deserve the guidance."     (28: 56)

The sole function of the prophet was to deliver Quran without
any alteration, addition, reduction, or explanation.

Please see pages  29-35.

## THE TRUE LOVE OF MUHAMMAD

The true love of Jesus is to recognize him as a human and
a messenger of God. The Christians love Jesus so much,
yet he disowns them on the Day of Judgment (Matthews 7: 23
and Quran 5: 116).

The true love of Muhammad is to recognize him as a human
and to follow his teachings, i.e., UPHOLD QURAN AND
NOTHING BUT QURAN. Those who follow "Hadith & Sunna"
are named as Muhammad's enemies, and Muhammad disowns them on the Day of Judgment as we see below:

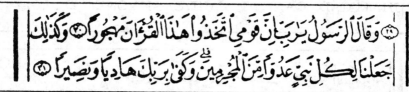

"(On the day of judgment) the messenger will say, 'My Lord;
my people have deserted THIS QURAN.' We thus set up
against every prophet enemies from among the guilty. Your
LORD SUFFICES AS A GUIDE AND SUPPORTER."
(25: 30-31)

-------------------------------------------------------------

Please note the "word for word" similarity between verse
31 above, and verse 112 of Sura 6 which deals specifically
with "Hadith."

-------------------------------------------------------------

God is the one who created you; God is the one who provides
for you; God is the one who terminates your life; God is the
one who resurrects you; God is the one who calls you to
account. Muhammad does none of these things (see 30: 40).

# MUHAMMAD DOES NOT KNOW THE FUTURE

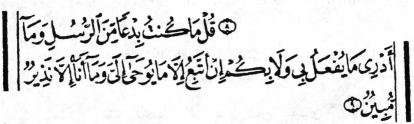

(46: 9)

"Say (O Muhammad), 'I do not bring anything new that is different from any other messenger. I have no idea what may happen to me, or to you. I simply follow what is revealed to me. I am no more than a manifest warner.'"

"Say (O Muhammad), 'I possess no power to benefit or harm even myself, except in accordance with God's will. (Nor do I know the future); had I known the future, I would have increased my wealth, and no harm would have afflicted me. I am no more than a warner, as well as bearer of good news for those who believe.'" (7: 188)

## MUHAMMAD DOES NOT KNOW THE FUTURE

Yet, hundreds of "Hadiths" narrate future events that have nothing to do with Quran, and represent personal prediction

---

One of the most prominent "Hadiths" is shown below:

" عليكم بسنتى وسنة الخلفاء الراشدين من بعدى " (حديث صحيح)

"You shall uphold my Sunna (traditions), and the Sunna of the 'guided Khalifas' (Al-Khulafaa' Al-Rashideen) who will come after me."

---

It should be noted that the expression "Al-Khulafaa' Al-Rashideen الخلفاء الراشدين " did not appear in Arabic literature until 200 years after the prophet; it is a modern expression.

How did the prophet know that there will be "Khulafaa'" who will succeed him, and how did he know that they will be called "Al-Khulafaa' Al-Rashideen" ?

---

The expression "Al-Khulafaa' Al-Rashideen" refers specifically to the four Khalifas: Abu Bakr, Umar, Uthman, and Ali. It was not known for two centuries after the prophet.

## THE MYTH OF INTERCESSION

Intercession is one of Satan's most effective tricks to dupe the people into idolizing their prophets and/or saints.

Although the Quran repeatedly states that there will be no intercession on the day of judgment, many Muslims were duped, through "Hadith & Sunna" into idolizing the prophet Muhammad against his will, and inventing the concept of INTERCESSION (Shafaa'ah):

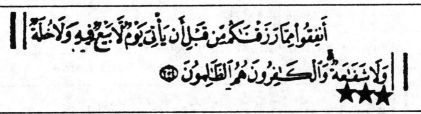

"Spend from our provisions to you before a day comes wherein there will be no trade, no nepotism, and NO INTER-CESSION." (2: 254)

"The prophets simply follow the commandments of God. He knows their past and future. THEY CANNOT INTERCEDE EXCEPT ON BEHALF OF THOSE ALREADY SAVED BY GOD. The prophets themselves worry about their own fate." (21: 28)

# THE DEIFICATION OF MUHAMMAD

# THE MYTH OF INTERCESSION

Despite the Quran's repeated assertions that Muhammad possesses no power to benefit anyone or harm anyone (see Page 25, & Page 30), Satan succeeded in duping many people through the concept of intercession. Satan convinced his victims that Muhammad will actually take them out of hell, and admit them into heaven!

Many so-called "Muslims" extend the concept of intercession to include numerous saints and/or imams:

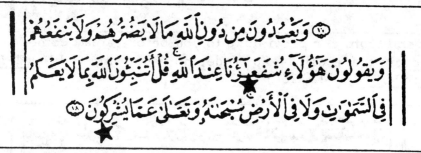

"They idolize beside God those who possess no power to harm them or benefit them, and say, 'These are our intercessors at God.' Say, 'Are you informing God of something He does not know in the heavens or the earth?' Glory be to Him; He is much too high to have any partners." (10: 18)

# THE DEIFICATION OF MUHAMMAD

## THE MYTH OF <u>MUHAMMAD THE INTERCESSOR</u>

The concept of intercession implies that God has some partners who intercede with Him on behalf of people.

Therefore, intercession is idol worship, and those who believe that Muhammad will intercede on behalf of anyone are idolizing the Prophet against his will. Intercession by Muhammad is prevalent in the Satanic innovations known as <u>Hadith</u> and/or <u>Sunna</u>.

The Quran clearly identifies intercession as idol worship, and declares a <u>GREAT CRITERION</u>; that those who believe in intercession cannot stand to talk about God <u>alone</u>; THEY HAVE TO MENTION THEIR IDOLS ALONG.

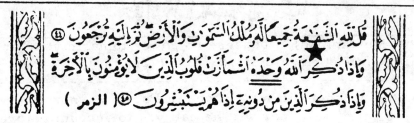

"Say, 'To God belongs ALL INTERCESSION. To Him belongs the dominion of the heavens and the earth, then to Him you will be returned.' When GOD ALONE is advocated, the hearts of those who do not believe in the hereafter shrink with aversion. But when idols are mentioned along with Him, they become satisfied." ( 39: 45 )

## MUHAMMAD WILL NOT CALL YOU TO ACCOUNT

فَإِنَّمَا عَلَيْكَ ٱلْبَلَاغُ وَعَلَيْنَا ٱلْحِسَابُ ۝

"Your ONLY mission (O Muhammad) is to deliver (Quran),
while it is we who will call them to account." (13: 40)

## MUHAMMAD CANNOT BENEFIT YOU OR HARM YOU

قُل لَّآ أَمْلِكُ لِنَفْسِى ضَرًّا وَلَا نَفْعًا ۝

"Say (O Muhammad),'I possess no power to harm myself, or
benefit myself.'"     (10: 49)

قُلْ إِنِّى لَآ أَمْلِكُ لَكُمْ ضَرًّا وَلَا رَشَدًا ۝

"Say (O Muhammad),'I possess no power to harm you, or
benefit you through guiding you.'"    (72: 21)

------------------------------------------------

Thus, the prophet will not put you in Paradise, nor can he
take you out of hell, nor will he call you to account before
him, nor can he benefit you, nor can he harm you; HIS
SOLE MISSION WAS DELIVERING QURAN, & NOTHING
BUT QURAN.  To love him and honor him is to follow Quran
alone, and reject the fabrications attributed to him.

## FUNCTION OF EVERY MESSENGER
## YOU SHALL NOT WORSHIP EXCEPT GOD

Neither Jesus, nor Muhammad, want to be idolized. Their
sole function was to preach the worship of GOD ALONE.

(سورة الأنبياء) ۞ وَمَا أَرْسَلْنَا مِن قَبْلِكَ مِن رَّسُولٍ
إِلَّا نُوحِى إِلَيْهِ أَنَّهُ لَا إِلَهَ إِلَّا أَنَا فَاعْبُدُونِ ۞ وَقَالُوا
اتَّخَذَ الرَّحْمَنُ وَلَدًا سُبْحَانَهُ بَلْ عِبَادٌ مُّكْرَمُونَ ۞
لَا يَسْبِقُونَهُ بِالْقَوْلِ وَهُم بِأَمْرِهِ يَعْمَلُونَ ۞ يَعْلَمُ مَا بَيْنَ
أَيْدِيهِمْ وَمَا خَلْفَهُمْ وَلَا يَشْفَعُونَ إِلَّا لِمَنِ ارْتَضَى وَهُم
مِّنْ خَشْيَتِهِ مُشْفِقُونَ ۞ وَمَن يَقُلْ مِنْهُمْ إِنِّي إِلَهٌ مِّن
دُونِهِ فَذَلِكَ نَجْزِيهِ جَهَنَّمَ كَذَلِكَ نَجْزِي الظَّالِمِينَ ۞

"Every messenger we sent before you was instructed to
preach that there is no god except Me; you shall worship
Me alone. Then they said,'God most gracious has begot-
ten a son.' Glory be to Him; all the messengers are no
more than honored servants. They do not speak on their
own; they simply follow His commands. He knows their
past and their future, and they possess no power to intercede except on behalf of those already approved by God.
The messengers themselves are worried about their own
fate. And, if any of them claims to be a god beside God,
we will punish him in hell; we thus punish the wicked."

(21:25-29)

---

| SOLE FUNCTION OF THE PROPHET: <u>DELIVER QURAN</u> |
| --- |

Repeatedly, the Quran employs "the double negative" to emphasize that Muhammad had <u>NO</u> function <u>EXCEPT</u> delivering Quran:

إِنْ عَلَيْكَ إِلَّا الْبَلَغُ

"You have <u>NO</u> duty <u>EXCEPT</u> delivering (Quran)" (42: 48)

فَإِنَّمَا عَلَيْكَ الْبَلَغُ وَعَلَيْنَا الْحِسَابُ ۞

"Your <u>ONLY</u> duty is delivering (Quran), while we will call them to account." (13: 40)

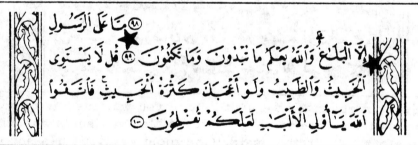

"The messenger has <u>NO</u> function <u>EXCEPT</u> delivering (Quran) and God knows whatever you declare, as well as whatever you conceal. Say, 'The good and the bad are not the same, despite the abundance of the bad.' Therefore, you shall observe God, O you who possess intelligence, that you may succeed." (5: 99-100)

- - - - - - - - - - - - - - - - - - - - - - - - - - - - - - - - - - - -

Unfortunately, those who refuse to believe that Quran is the <u>ONLY SOURCE OF RELIGIOUS GUIDANCE</u> are much more abundant than those who believe.
(see also 16:35, 82; 24:54; 29:18; 36:17;& 64:12)

## MUHAMMAD DOES NOT EXPLAIN, INTERPRET, OR ANTICIPATE QURAN; JUST <u>DELIVER</u> & <u>FOLLOW</u>.

<u>Hadith</u> & <u>Sunna</u> advocates claim that <u>Hadith</u> & <u>Sunna</u> are needed to explain Quran.

However, Quran teaches that God is the teacher of Quran; that God will put Quran into the hearts of believers regardless of their mother tongue; and that Muhammad will not explain Quran. Documents are shown below:

God is the teacher of Quran (55: 1-2)

"Whether it came down in non-Arabic or Arabic, say, 'For those who believe, it is a guidance and healing. As for the disbelievers, they will be deaf and blind to it.'"(41: 44)

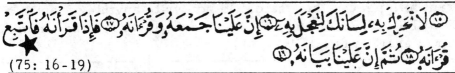

(75: 16-19)

"Do not move your tongue (O Muhammad) in anticipation of Quran. It is we who put it together as a Quran. Once we recite it, <u>you shall follow it</u>. Then, <u>it is we who explain it</u>."

---

## THE FOLLOWERS OF HADITH & SUNNA

## DO NOT FOLLOW THEIR OWN TEACHINGS

---

The most authoritative books of Hadith, namely, Muslim &
Ibn Hanbal, report that the Prophet ordered that no one shall
take anything from him EXCEPT QURAN. Shown below is
the Arabic text of this Hadith:

---

«السابع ـ النهى عن كتابة غير القرآن»

عَنْ أَبِى سَعِيدٍ الْخُدْرِىّ رَضِىَ اللهُ عَنْهُ قَالَ : قَالَ رَسُولُ اللهِ صَلَّى اللهُ

عَلَيْهِ وَسَلَّمَ : «لَاتَكْتُبُوا عَنِّى شَيْئاً سِوَى الْقُرْآنِ . مَنْ كَتَبَ شَيْئاً

سِوَى الْقُرْآنِ فَلْيَمْحُهُ»(١) .

(احمد ج ١ ص ١٧١ ومسلم)

---

"Abi Saeed Al-Khudry - may God be pleased with him -
reported that the messenger of God - may God exalt him &
grant him peace - had said, 'Do not write anything from me
EXCEPT QURAN. Anyone who wrote anything other than
Quran shall erase it.'"     !!!

---

Thus, according to their own teachings,

---

## THEY     DISOBEY     THE     PROPHET

---

## INCREDIBLE FACT:
## THEY DO NOT FOLLOW THEIR OWN TEACHINGS

According to the most "authoritative" sources of
<u>Hadith</u>, the Prophet never changed his mind about writing
from him ONLY QURAN:

عَنْ عَبْدِ الْمُطَّلِبِ بْنِ عَبْدِ اللهِ قَالَ : [دَخَلَ زَيْدُ بْنُ ثَابِتٍ رَضِيَ اللهُ

عَنْهُ عَلَى مُعَاوِيَةَ رَضِيَ اللهُ عَنْهُ ، فَحَدَّثَهُ حَدِيثاً ، فَأَمَرَ إِنْسَاناً أَنْ يَكْتُبَ .

فَقَالَ زَيْدٌ : إِنَّ رَسُولَ اللهِ صَلَّى اللهُ عَلَيْهِ وَسَلَّمَ نَهَى أَنْ نَكْتُبَ شَيْئاً

مِنْ حَدِيثِهِ ، فَمَحَاهُ ] .

( أحمد ج ١ ص ١٩٢ )

Zayd Ibn Thabit (the Prophet's closest revelation writer)
visited the Khalifa Mu'aawiyah (more than 30 years after
the Prophet's death), and told him a story about the Prophet. Mu'aawiyah liked the story and ordered someone
to write it down. But Zayd said, "The messenger of God
ordered us never to write anything of his Hadith."
(reported by Ibn Hanbal)

THEY DISOBEY THEIR OWN FABRICATED IDOL !!

## QURAN: DO THEY HAVE A "BOOK" WHERE THEY FIND ANYTHING THEY WISH?

When you confront the followers of Hadith & Sunna with the Hadith shown on the previous page, they admit the existence of such Hadith. They explain their failure to follow their own teachings by the fact that there exist equally "authentic" Hadiths where the Prophet ordered the writing of his Hadiths!!

The Quran describes such people as "criminals", and asks:"Do they have a 'Book' where they can find anything they wish???"

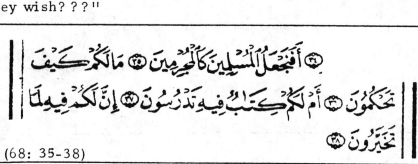

(68: 35-38)

"Shall we treat the Muslims like the criminals? What is wrong with your judgment? DO YOU HAVE A BOOK WHERE YOU CAN FIND ANYTHING YOU WISH?"

-----------------------------------------------------------

Both Hadith and Sunna fit this Quranic description; as a "Book where you can find anything you wish."

-----------------------------------------------------------

The conjectural and contradictory nature of Hadith and Sunna are unanimously recognized.

-----------------------------------------------------------

# THEIR FAVORITE QUESTION

---

## "If Quran is complete and fully detailed (as God says), where can we find the details of Salat prayers?"

---

This famous question reveals **their total ignorance of Quran** and a subconcious effort to prove that God is wrong in His repeated assertions that Quran is "complete" and "fully detailed".

For the Quran teaches in no uncertain terms that Abraham is the founder of Islam as it is practiced today. As such, what did Abraham contribute to our daily life as Muslims?

---

The Quran teaches that **ALL RELIGIOUS PRACTICES IN ISLAM (Salat, Zakat, Fasting & Hajj) CAME TO US FROM ABRAHAM, GENERATION AFTER GENERATION.**

Thus, Islam in its final form, as is practiced today, is based on two things:
(1) **QURAN:** contributed through Muhammad, and
(2) **RELIGIOUS PRACTICES:** through Abraham.

ALL RELIGIOUS PRACTICES IN ISLAM EXISTED BEFORE MUHAMMAD.

Muhammad's **SOLE FUNCTION** was to deliver Quran (see Pages 30-33).

## ABRAHAM: THE FOUNDER OF ISLAM

Abraham was the first recipient of the concept of ISLAM, and the first user of the word "MUSLIM" (see 2: 131).

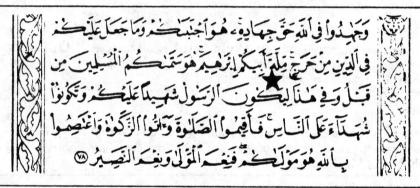

"You shall strive in the cause of God as you should. He has blessed you, and imposed no hardship in your religion; the RELIGION OF YOUR FATHER ABRAHAM. Abraham is the one who named you 'Muslims' in the beginning. Thus, the messenger serves as witness among you, just as you serve as witnesses among the people. Therefore, you shall observe the Salat prayers, give the Zakat charity, and hold fast to God; He is your Lord; the best Lord, and the best supporter." ( 22: 78 )

-------------------------------------------------

Thus, if Abraham is the founder of Islam, did he contribute anything to our Islamic life?

-------------------------------------------------

The answer is: "YES; he contributed THE RELIGIOUS PRACTICES (Salat, Zakat, Fasting, & Hajj)."

---

ISLAM IS THE RELIGION OF ABRAHAM

---

While Muhammad's mission, sole mission, was delivering Quran, ALL RELIGIOUS PRACTICES CAME THROUGH ABRAHAM.

---

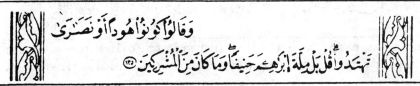

"They said,' Be you Jews or Christians in order to be guided.' Say, 'We follow the religion of Abraham, monotheism; he never was an idol-worshiper.'" (2:135)

- - - - - - - - - - - - - - - - - - - - - - - - - - - - - - -

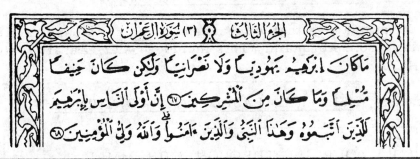

"Abraham was neither Jewish, nor Christian; he was a monotheist; a Muslim; he never was an idol-worshiper. The people most worthy of following Abraham are those who followed him, and this prophet (Muhammad), and those who believed.  God is the Lord of the believers."

(3:67-68)

---

---

MUHAMMAD WAS A FOLLOWER OF ABRAHAM

---

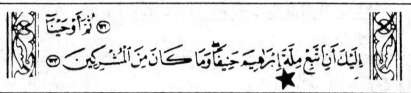

"Then we inspired you (O Muhammad) to follow the religion of Abraham, monotheism; never was he an idol-worshiper." (16: 123)

------------------------------------------------------------

Logically, if Muhammad was a follower of Abraham, and we are followers of Muhammad, then we are followers of Abraham. What did we learn from Abraham ? ? ?

------------------------------------------------------------

The Quran teaches that we learned all the religious practices of Islam from Abraham. This includes Salat, Zakat, fasting, and Hajj.

------------------------------------------------------------

Therefore, ISLAM IS BASED ON TWO THINGS:

 QURAN: THROUGH MUHAMMAD

 RELIGIOUS PRACTICES: VIA ABRAHAM

## SALAT PRACTICED BY MUHAMMAD'S OPPONENTS

The whole Arabian society before and during the time of Muhammad followed the religion of Abraham. Thus, Abu Lahab, Abu Jahl, and the idolators of Quraish used to observe the FIVE DAILY SALAT PRAYERS exactly as we do today, with the single exception of substituting the Quranic Faatihha for the Ibrahimy Faatihha.

------------------------------------------------------------

وَمَا كَانَ ٱللَّهُ لِيُعَذِّبَهُمْ وَأَنتَ فِيهِمْ وَمَا كَانَ ٱللَّهُ
مُعَذِّبَهُمْ وَهُمْ يَسْتَغْفِرُونَ ۝ وَمَا لَهُمْ أَلَّا يُعَذِّبَهُمُ ٱللَّهُ وَهُمْ يَصُدُّونَ
عَنِ ٱلْمَسْجِدِ ٱلْحَرَامِ وَمَا كَانُوٓا۟ أَوْلِيَآءَهُۥٓ إِنْ أَوْلِيَآؤُهُۥٓ إِلَّا ٱلْمُتَّقُونَ وَلَٰكِنَّ
أَكْثَرَهُمْ لَا يَعْلَمُونَ ۝ وَمَا كَانَ صَلَاتُهُمْ عِندَ ٱلْبَيْتِ إِلَّا مُكَآءً
وَتَصْدِيَةً فَذُوقُوا۟ ٱلْعَذَابَ بِمَا كُنتُمْ تَكْفُرُونَ ۝

------------------------------------------------------------

"God was not to punish them while you (Muhammad) were still among them. God was not to punish them while they are seeking forgiveness. Yet, they fully deserved God's punishment for repelling from the sacred mosque, though they were not the guardians thereof; only the righteous are guardians thereof, but most of them do not know. THEIR SALAT PRAYERS at the shrine were no more than deceit and repulsion. Therefore, suffer the retribution for your disbelief." ( 8: 33-35 )

------------------------------------------------------------

## SACRED MONTHS OBSERVED BEFORE MUHAMMAD

The four sacred months in Islam were observed before the
time of Muhammad. This further proves that all religious
practices of Islam were neither initiated, nor taught by the
Prophet Muhammad; his sole mission was to deliver Quran.

إِنَّ عِدَّةَ الشُّهُورِ عِندَ اللَّهِ اثْنَا عَشَرَ شَهْرًا فِي كِتَابِ اللَّهِ
يَوْمَ خَلَقَ السَّمَاوَاتِ وَالْأَرْضَ مِنْهَا أَرْبَعَةٌ حُرُمٌ ذَلِكَ الدِّينُ الْقَيِّمُ
فَلَا تَظْلِمُوا فِيهِنَّ أَنفُسَكُمْ وَقَاتِلُوا الْمُشْرِكِينَ كَافَّةً كَمَا يُقَاتِلُونَكُمْ
كَافَّةً وَاعْلَمُوا أَنَّ اللَّهَ مَعَ الْمُتَّقِينَ إِنَّمَا النَّسِيءُ زِيَادَةٌ فِي الْكُفْرِ
يُضَلُّ بِهِ الَّذِينَ كَفَرُوا يُحِلُّونَهُ عَامًا وَيُحَرِّمُونَهُ عَامًا لِيُوَاطِئُوا عِدَّةَ
مَا حَرَّمَ اللَّهُ فَيُحِلُّوا مَا حَرَّمَ اللَّهُ زُيِّنَ لَهُمْ سُوءُ أَعْمَالِهِمْ وَاللَّهُ لَا يَهْدِي
الْقَوْمَ الْكَافِرِينَ

"The count of months according to God is twelve, as shown
in God's scriptures, since the day He created the heavens
and the earth. Four of them are sacred. This is the right
religion; therefore, do not wrong your souls during the four
months. But you may fight the idolators, if they attack you
therein, and know that God is with the righteous. The practice of alternating the sacred months is a pagan practice.
Thus, they changed the sacred months, making them viol-
able one year and sacred the next year, as if to maintain
the count instituted by God......"   (9:36-37)

# TODAY'S IDOLATERS vs QURAISH'S IDOLATERS

Millions of "Muslims" today practice a form of idolatry that is similar to the idolatry of pre-Muhammad Quraish.

Millions of "Muslims" in Egypt, Iran, Pakistan, India, and many other countries go to the Mosque to pray. Their Salat prayers are definitely to God. After finishing their Salat, they visit the tomb of the saint and ask for health, wealth, and/or children.

The idol worshipers of Quraish observed the five Salat prayers exactly as we do today, but they also visited their idols Allat, Al-'Uzzah, Manat, etc., to ask for health, wealth, and/or children.

Thus, the flagrant idolatry practiced by millions of Muslims today is exactly identical to the idolatry of Quraish before and during the time of Muhammad; only the idols are different.

Except for the Jewish and Christian minorities, the Arabian society prior to the mission of Muhammad followed the religion of Abraham. They practiced all the religious duties of Islam. Their Salat prayers were identical to ours, but they also practiced idol-worship. The "Muslim" masses today practice idol-worship by idolizing the Prophet against his will, by idolizing their saints and holy men or imams, and following other sources beside Quran (see pages 7 & 8).

## " YOU SHALL KEEP THE OBSERVANCE OF SALAT"

This commandment was issued during the first few weeks of Quranic revelation.

DOES IT MAKE ANY SENSE THAT GOD WOULD ISSUE

A COMMANDMENT TO OBSERVE SOMETHING NOT AL-

READY KNOWN ? ? ?

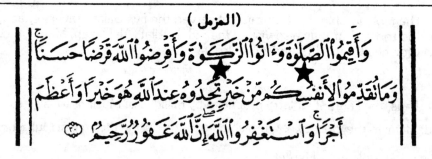

"... and keep the observance of Salat and Zakat, and lend to God a loan of righteousness. Whatever you advance for your souls, you will find at God better and multiplied manyfold. And seek God's forgiveness; God is forgiving, merciful." (73: 20)

- - - - - - - - - - - - - - - - - - - - - - - - - - - - - - - - - - - - - - - - - - -

The word "Salat" is very specific and means only one thing, i.e., the observance of specific practices involving bowing and prostration. This is true throughout Quran, throughout the ages, and in relation to any prophet, messenger, etc.

---

ALL RELIGIOUS PRACTICES IN ISLAM
( SALAT ZAKAT FASTING HAJJ )
CAME TO US THROUGH ABRAHAM

---

In 2: 128 we see Abraham and Ismail implore God to teach them "THE RELIGIOUS PRACTICES OF ISLAM."

---

وَإِذْ يَرْفَعُ إِبْرَاهِيمُ الْقَوَاعِدَ مِنَ الْبَيْتِ وَإِسْمَاعِيلُ رَبَّنَا تَقَبَّلْ مِنَّا إِنَّكَ أَنْتَ السَّمِيعُ الْعَلِيمُ رَبَّنَا وَاجْعَلْنَا مُسْلِمَيْنِ لَكَ وَمِن ذُرِّيَّتِنَا أُمَّةً مُّسْلِمَةً لَّكَ وَأَرِنَا مَنَاسِكَنَا وَتُبْ عَلَيْنَا إِنَّكَ أَنْتَ التَّوَّابُ الرَّحِيمُ

★★★

---

"As Abraham raised the foundations of Kaaba, together with Ismail, they prayed, 'Our Lord, accept this work from us; you are the hearer, the omniscient. Our Lord, & make us Muslims to you; and from our descendants let there be a nation of Muslims to you; AND TEACH US HOW TO PRACTICE OUR RELIGIOUS DUTIES, and redeem us; you are the redeemer, the merciful.'" (2:127-128)

---

---

### ABRAHAM: FIRST (and last) RECIPIENT OF SPECIFIC RELIGIOUS PRACTICES.

---

The prophets and messengers prior to Abraham were not given any religious practices. The human society was so primitive, only BELIEF IN GOD ALONE was all that is required for salvation. See for example Sura 71, entitled "Noah." Thus, RELIGIOUS PRACTICES appear in Quran ONLY after Abraham; never before him.

---

(2:43) وَأَقِيمُوا الصَّلَوٰةَ وَءَاتُوا الزَّكَوٰةَ وَارْكَعُوا مَعَ الرَّاكِعِينَ ۩

"(O Children of Israel,)you shall observe the Salat prayers & Zakat charity; you shall bow down with those who bow."

---

وَإِذْ جَعَلْنَا الْبَيْتَ مَثَابَةً لِّلنَّاسِ وَأَمْنًا وَاتَّخِذُوا مِن مَّقَامِ إِبْرَاهِـمَ مُصَلًّى وَعَهِدْنَا إِلَىٰ إِبْرَاهِـمَ وَإِسْمَاعِيلَ أَن طَهِّرَا بَيْتِىَ لِلطَّائِفِينَ وَالْعَاكِفِينَ وَالرُّكَّعِ السُّجُودِ ۩

"We made the Kaaba a focal point for all the people, and a sanctuary; thus, you shall consider this station of Abraham a place of worship. And we appointed Abraham and Ismail to purify My shrine for those who would visit it, those who would retreat therein, and those who bow and prostrate."

(2: 125)

## SALAT PRAYERS OBSERVED BEFORE MUHAMMAD

But the Jews and Christians "LOST" the Salat prayers.

يَمَرْيَمُ اقْنُتِى لِرَبِّكِ وَاسْجُدِى وَارْكَعِى مَعَ الرَّاكِعِينَ

"O Mary, you shall obey your Lord, and you shall prostrate and bow down with those who bow down." (3: 43) ★

قَالَ إِنِّى عَبْدُ اللهِ آتَانِىَ الْكِتَابَ وَجَعَلَنِى نَبِيًّا وَجَعَلَنِى مُبَارَكًا أَيْنَ مَا كُنْتُ وَأَوْصَانِى بِالصَّلَوةِ وَالزَّكَوةِ مَا دُمْتُ حَيًّا

"(Jesus said,) God has made me blessed wherever I go, and He commanded me to observe the Salat prayers and Zakat charity for as long as I live." (19: 31)

فَخَلَفَ مِنْ بَعْدِهِمْ خَلْفٌ أَضَاعُوا الصَّلَوةَ وَاتَّبَعُوا الشَّهَوَاتِ

"Generations came thereafter who LOST the Salat prayers, and pursued their lusts." (19: 59)

- - - - - - - - - - - - - - - - - - - - - - - - - - - - - - - - - - -

There are remnants of the Salat prayers among the Jews, namely, the Samaritans, and the Christians (the Russian Orthodox Church). It is noteworthy that the Samaritan Jews have denounced the man-made commandments of Talmud, and decided to adhere to the word of God alone, i.e., Torah (see "The Myth of God Incarnate", Page 117).

---

## SALAT & ZAKAT CAME TO US VIA ABRAHAM

---

Those who refuse to believe God are challenging Quran by asking, "If Quran is complete and fully detailed (as stated in 6: 19, 38, & 114), where can we find the details of Salat and Zakat?" For such people, who are obviously isolated from Quran (see 18: 57), we present the following Quranic truth:

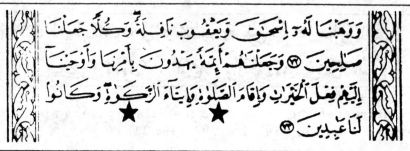

"And we granted him (Abraham) Isaac and Jacob as a gift, and we made them righteous. And we appointed them imams who guided in accordance with our commandments, AND WE TAUGHT THEM RIGHTEOUS WORKS AND THE OBSERVANCE OF SALAT AND ZAKAT." ( 21: 72-73)

- - - - - - - - - - - - - - - - - - - - - - - - - - - - - - - - - - - - - - - - -

Unfortunately, this plain Quranic truth is not accessible by those who keep trying to prove that Quran is not complete.

FIRST, they have to come to sincere conviction that Quran is complete, perfect, and fully detailed; they have to believe their Lord. Once they attain this conviction, the shields will be removed from around their hearts, the deafness will be removed from their ears, and they will become worthy of the Quranic truth.

## FASTING CAME TO US VIA ABRAHAM

(then modified in Quran)

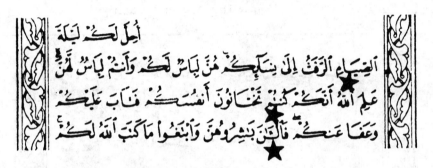

"You are permitted to have sexual intercourse with your wives during the night of fasting; they are your confidantes, and you are their confidants. God knew that YOU USED TO BETRAY YOUR SOULS (by having intercourse during the night) IN THE PAST. He has redeemed you, and He has pardoned you. HENCEFORTH, you may have intercourse with them, seeking what God has permitted for you." (part of 2:187)

- - - - - - - - - - - - - - - - - - - - - - - - - - - - - - - - - - - - - - - - - - -

This verse, therefore, clearly informs us that fasting was practiced before Muhammad according to the religion of Abraham (Islam).

- - - - - - - - - - - - - - - - - - - - - - - - - - - - - - - - - - - - - - - - - - -

When fasting was initially ordained through Abraham, sexual intercourse was prohibited throughout the fasting month of Ramadan, day and night.

## HAJJ CAME TO US VIA ABRAHAM

Please note that the same verse also shows THE METHOD

OF SALAT PRAYER ( bowing & prostrating ):

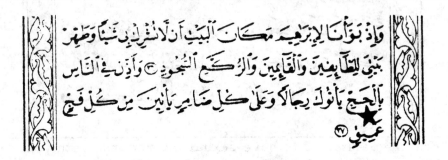

"We pointed out to Abraham the location of the shrine, and directed him to worship none beside Me, and to purify My shrine for those who would visit it, those who would retreat therein, and those who would bow and prostrate. And you shall declare (O Abraham) that the people shall observe Hajj. They will then come to you, walking or riding, from the farthest places." (22: 26-27)

------------------------------------------------------------

Thus, Quran clearly teaches that ALL RELIGIOUS PRACTICES IN ISLAM (Salat, Zakat, Fasting, & Hajj) came to us via Abraham .

------------------------------------------------------------

Quran teaches that God taught Abraham how to do Salat, Zakat, Fasting, & Hajj, then Abraham taught these practices to his children, and so on generation after generation.

## THEY STILL INSIST

Even after showing all this Quranic evidence to those who do not believe God, you will note that they insist on their ways. Do not be surprised if they ask you after all this:"Where are the details of Salat prayers in Quran?"

-----------------------------------------------------------------

Until they decide to believe their Creator in His repeated assertions that Quran is complete, they can never see the Quranic truth. This is documented below:

## CONSEQUENCES OF REFUSING TO BELIEVE QURAN

Deprivation from seeing, hearing, or understanding Quran. Thus, guidance becomes impossible:

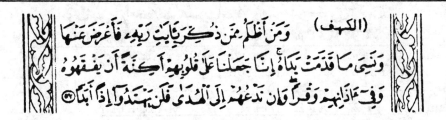

"Who is more wicked than one who is reminded of the verses of his Lord, then disregards them, while unaware of his sin? Consequently, we place shields on their hearts, to prevent them from understanding (Quran), and deafness in their ears. Thus, if you invite them to the guidance, they can never ever be guided." ( 18: 57 )

-----------------------------------------------------------------

## TWO UNFORTUNATE FACTS OF LIFE

(1) The majority of people are disbelievers.

(2) The majority of BELIEVERS are going to hell.

وَمَا أَكْثَرُ النَّاسِ وَلَوْ حَرَصْتَ بِمُؤْمِنِينَ ۝

"The majority of people, no matter what you do, are not believers."          ( 12: 103 )

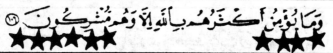

وَمَا يُؤْمِنُ أَكْثَرُهُم بِاللَّهِ إِلَّا وَهُم مُّشْرِكُونَ ۝

"And the majority of those who believe in God are idol-worshipers."          ( 12: 106 )

-----------------------------------------------

Thus, IF YOU ARE WITH THE MAJORITY, YOU ARE IN DEEP TROUBLE.

-----------------------------------------------

Even if you are with the majority of BELIEVERS, you are in deep trouble.

-----------------------------------------------

Those who worship GOD ALONE are a rare and extremely fortunate group; they are a minority of the minority.

## PROBLEM IS: THEY THINK THEY ARE RIGHTEOUS

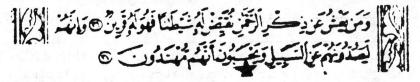

"Anyone who disregards the message of God most gracious, we appoint a devil to be his constant companion. The devils then divert them from the path, yet make them THINK that they are rightly guided." (43: 36-37)

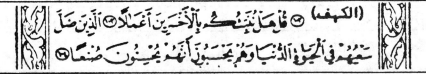

"You shall be strictly righteous at every mosque, and worship God, devoting your worship absolutely to Him alone. Just as He created you initially, you will be returned. Some He guides. Others are committed to straying, for they take the devils as allies instead of God, and THINK that they are rightly guided." (7: 29-30)

The worst losers are those who go astray, then THINK that they are rightly guided. (18: 103-104)

## UNAWARE OF THEIR IDOL WORSHIP

The majority of "believers" fall into idol-worship without realizing it; they are not aware that they are idolators:

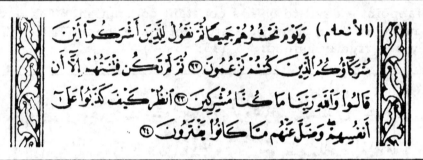

"On the day (of judgment) when we gather all the people, we will ask the idol-worshipers, 'Where are your idols whom you set up beside God?' Then, their only answer will be, 'By God our Lord, we were not idol-worshipers.' Note how they lied even to themselves, and note that the idols they had set up will abandon them."     (6: 22-24)

- - - - - - - - - - - - - - - - - - - - - - - - - - - - - - - - - - - - - - - - - - - - - - - - - - - - -

Thus, there are people who are idol-worshipers, who are unaware of their idolatry.  Could you be one of them?  How do you know that you are not one of them?  This is your only chance to ascertain that you are not an idol-worshiper.

- - - - - - - - - - - - - - - - - - - - - - - - - - - - - - - - - - - - - - - - - - - - - - - - - - - - -

HOW CAN YOU ASCERTAIN THAT YOU ARE NOT AN

IDOL-WORSHIPER ?   The answer on Page 55.

## THE IMPORTANCE OF "HADITH & SUNNA"

Quran teaches that "Hadith & Sunna" constitute the necessary test to distinguish the true Muslim from the false Muslim.

- - - - - - - - - - - - - - - - - - - - - - - - - - - - - - - - - - - - - - - - - - - - -

The true Muslim believes God in His statements that Quran is complete, perfect, and fully detailed (6: 19, 38, & 114). Consequently, the true Muslim does not accept any other source for religious guidance.

- - - - - - - - - - - - - - - - - - - - - - - - - - - - - - - - - - - - - - - - - - - - -

As for the false Muslim, he or she will become attracted to "Hadith & Sunna", and thus exposed as a hypocrite who utters belief, while the heart inside is denying (see 16: 22).

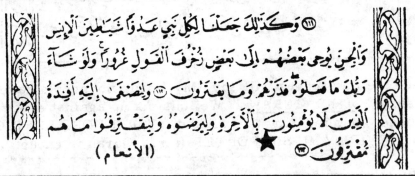

"We set up against every prophet enemies, human and jinn devils, who exhort each other to invent fancy statements in order to deceive. Had your Lord willed, they would not have done it. (But it is God's will) in order that the minds of those who do not believe in the hereafter may listen thereto, and to let them accept it, and to expose their true identity."     (6: 112-113)

- - - - - - - - - - - - - - - - - - - - - - - - - - - - - - - - - - - - - - - - - - - - -

Are you satisfied with the Quran? Do you believe God? Or, do you feel that Quran is not complete; that you need additional sources of religious guidance?

## ONE AUTHENTIC "HADITH"

On the day of judgment, Muhammad will be the first to complain that his followers had abandoned Quran, in favor of the fabrications by his enemies (Hadith & Sunna):

(25: 30-31)

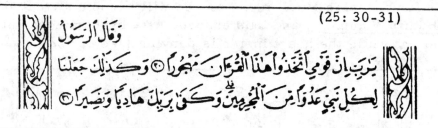

"And the messenger will say, 'My Lord, my people have deserted THIS QURAN.' We thus set up against every prophet enemies who are wicked. YOUR LORD SUFFICES AS A GUIDE AND SUPPORTER (i.e., Quran is enough)."

Note the word for word similarity between 25:31 shown above, and 6: 112 shown on the previous page. Could this be coincidental?

Thus, the prophet Muhammad will be disappointed with those who love him excessively, just as Jesus will be disappointed with those Christians who considered him to be a god or son of God.

## QURAN: THE ONLY LEGITIMATE " HADITH "

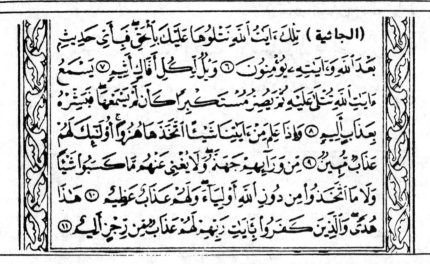

"These are God's verses; we recite them for you truthfully.
In which "Hadith", beside God and His verses, do they believe in? <u>WOE TO EVERY SINFUL FABRICATOR</u>. He hears
God's verses, then insists arrogantly on his way, as if he
never heard them; promise him painful retribution. When he
learns anything from our verses, he takes it in vain; these
have deserved humiliating retribution. Awaiting them is hell;
neither their earnings, nor the idols they had set up beside
God can help them; they have deserved terrible retribution.
<u>THIS IS THE GUIDANCE</u>, and those who do not believe the
verses of their Lord will suffer debasement, and painful
retribution. " ( 45: 6-11 )

- - - - - - - - - - - - - - - - - - - - - - - - - - - - - - - - - - - - -

Do you believe God's verses? Do you believe that Quran is
complete, perfect, and fully detailed (6: 19, 38, & 114)? Or,
do you have to have other sources beside Quran?

Quran is the only "Hadith" to be followed; all other Hadiths are blasphemous and misleading fabrications:

(39: 23)

اللهُ نَزَّلَ أَحْسَنَ الْحَدِيثِ كِتَابًا مُتَشَابِهًا مَثَانِيَ تَقْشَعِرُّ مِنْهُ جُلُودُ الَّذِينَ يَخْشَوْنَ رَبَّهُمْ ثُمَّ تَلِينُ جُلُودُهُمْ وَقُلُوبُهُمْ إِلَى ذِكْرِ اللَّهِ ذَلِكَ هُدَى اللَّهِ يَهْدِي بِهِ مَن يَشَاءُ وَمَن يُضْلِلِ اللَّهُ فَمَا لَهُ مِنْ هَادٍ ۩

"God has revealed the best 'Hadith'; a book that is consistent, and describes both ways (to heaven and Hell). The skins of those who reverence their Lord shudder therefrom, then their skins and hearts soften up and receive God's message. Such is God's guidance; He guides whomever He wills. As for those sent astray by Him, no one can guide them."

وَمِنَ النَّاسِ مَن يَشْتَرِي لَهْوَ الْحَدِيثِ لِيُضِلَّ عَن سَبِيلِ اللَّهِ بِغَيْرِ عِلْمٍ وَيَتَّخِذَهَا هُزُوًا أُولَئِكَ لَهُمْ عَذَابٌ مُّهِينٌ ۞ وَإِذَا تُتْلَى عَلَيْهِ آيَاتُنَا وَلَّى مُسْتَكْبِرًا كَأَن لَّمْ يَسْمَعْهَا كَأَنَّ فِي أُذُنَيْهِ وَقْرًا فَبَشِّرْهُ بِعَذَابٍ أَلِيمٍ ۞

"There are those who advocate vain 'Hadith' causing diversion from the path of God, without knowledge, and fail to take such actions seriously; these have deserved humiliating retribution. And when our verses are recited to him, he turns away arrogantly, as if he never heard them; as if his ears are deaf; promise him painful retribution." (31: 6-7)

# THE PHYSICAL EVIDENCE

In addition to the clear Quranic statements assuring the believers that Quran is complete; perfect, fully detailed, and shall be the **ONLY** source of religious guidance, it was the will of God Almighty to further support these revelations with irrefutable **PHYSICAL EVIDENCE.**

- - - - - - - - - - - - - - - - - - - - - - - - - - - - - - - - - - - - - - - - - -

A mathematical miracle was discovered in Quran, whereby every word, indeed every letter, was placed in Quran in accordance with an extremely intricate numerical code. The code is based on the number [19], which is the number of letters in the opening statement of Quran, and the number indicated in 74: 30 as providing the answer to those who claim that Quran is man-made. This mathematical miracle proves beyond doubt that Quran is a divine scripture, and that it has been perfectly preserved. For details please see the book, **"QURAN: VISUAL PRESENTATION OF THE MIRACLE."**

- - - - - - - - - - - - - - - - - - - - - - - - - - - - - - - - - - - - - - - - - -

The **PHYSICAL EVIDENCE** supporting Quran as **THE ONLY SOURCE OF RELIGIOUS GUIDANCE** is interlocking with the mathematical miracle of Quran; it is also based on the number [19]. Such evidence is presented on pages 64-72.

- - - - - - - - - - - - - - - - - - - - - - - - - - - - - - - - - - - - - - - - - -

Since the evidence is purely PHYSICAL, rather than interpretative, all free-thinking people will accept it. Only those hopelessly trapped in false convictions will fail to see the clear truth, due to the curse of rejecting Quran (see 17: 45).

- - - - - - - - - - - - - - - - - - - - - - - - - - - - - - - - - - - - - - - - - -

The following four pages summarizing the miracle of Quran are reprinted from the book: **"QURAN: VISUAL PRESENTATION OF THE MIRACLE."**

# QURAN: VISUAL PRESENTATION OF THE MIRACLE

by

Rashad Khalifa, Ph.D.
Imam, Mosque of Tucson, Arizona

## SUMMARY & CONCLUSIONS

The miracle of Quran detailed in this book ranges from extreme simplicity to extreme intricacy. Because Quran was sent down for **ALL** people, its language ranges from the very simple, to the highest levels of linguistic and literary excellence. This renders the message attainable by everyone, regardless of the level of education. The same is true with the Quran's miracle. Thus, the physical facts that make up this extraordinary phenomenon can be divided into **SIMPLE FACTS** and **INTRICATE FACTS**.

## THE SIMPLE FACTS

(1) The opening statement of Quran consists of 19 letters.
(2) Quran consists of 114 chapters, or 6 x 19.
(3) The first Quranic revelation (96:1-5) was 19 words.
(4) First revelation consisted of 76 letters, or 19 x 4.
(5) First chapter revealed (Ch. 96) consists of 19 verses.
(6) From the end of Quran, Ch. 96 is in position 19.
(7) First chapter revealed consists of 304 letters; 19 x 16.
(8) Last chapter revealed (Ch. 110) consists of 19 words.
(9) First verse of last revelation consists of 19 letters.
(10) Second revelation (68:1-9) was 38 words; 19 x 2.
(11) Third revelation (73:1-10) was 57 words; 19 x 3.
(12) Fourth revelation (74:1-30) brought the No. 19 itself.
(13) Fifth revelation (Ch. 1) placed the 19-lettered opening statement immediately after the No. 19 of 74:30.

## SUMMARY & CONCLUSTIONS (cont'd):

(14) First word in the opening statement occurs in Quran exactly 19 times.

(15) Second word in the opening statement (Allah) occurs 2,698 times, a multiple of 19 (19 x 142).

(16) Third word in the opening statement (Rahman) is mentioned in Quran 57 times (19 x 3).

(17) Fourth word in the opening statement (Rahim) is mentioned in Quran 114 times (19 x 6).

(18) Multiplication factors of the opening statement (see points 14-17 above) [1+142+3+6] add up to a total of 152, which is also a multiple of 19 (19 x 8).

(19) Each frequency of occurence connected with the opening statement, i.e., 19, 2698, 57, & 114 corresponds to the numerical value of one of God's names.

(20) All compiled lists of the known names of God (more than 400) were found to include **ONLY FOUR** names with numerical values divisible by 19. These four names are the same four which correspond to the frequencies of occurence mentioned in point 19 above.

(21) Opening statement is missing from Chapter 9, but compensated in Chapter 27, verse 30. This restores the frequency of this crucial statement to 114 (19 x 6).

(22) Between the missing statement (Chapter 9) and the extra statement (Chapter 27) there are 19 chapters.

## THE INTRICATE FACTS

(23) Chapter 50 is entitled "Q," initialed with the letter "Q," and contains 57 Q's (57=19x3).

(24) The only other chapter initialed with "Q," namely, Chapter 42, also contains 57 Q's (19 x 3).

(25) The letter "Q" stands for "Quran," and the total occurence of "Q" in the two Q-initialed chapters equals the number of chapters in Quran (57+57=114).

## Summary & Conclusions (cont'd):

(26) First verse in Chapter 50 (entitled "Q") describes Quran as "Majeed = Glorious," and the numerical value of the word "Majeed" is 57, exactly the same as the number of Q's in this chapter.

(27) Chapter 68 is initialed with the letter "N" and contains 133 N's; or 19 x 7.

(28) Chapters 7, 19, & 38 are initialed with the letter "S" (Saad), and the total frequency of occurence of this letter in the three chapters is 152, or 19 x 8.

(29) Chapter 36 is initialed with the letters "Y" & "S," and the total frequency of these two letters in this chapter is 285, or 19 x 15.

(30) Chapters 40 through 46 are initialed with "H" and "M." The total frequency of these two letters in the seven chapters is 2147, or 19 x 113.

(31) Chapter 42 is prefixed with the three initials "'A," "S," & "Q," and the total occurrence of these three letters in this chapter is 209, or 19 x 11.

(32) Chapter 19 is initialed with five letters, namely, "K," "H," "Y," "'A," and "S," and the total frequency of occurrence of these five letters in this chapter is 798, or 19 x 42.

(33) The Quranic initials "H," "T.H.," "T.S." and T.S.M." constitute a unique interlocking relationship within their five chapters, namely, 19, 20, 26, 27, & 28. The total frequency of occurrence of these letters in their five chapters is 1767, or 19 x 93.

(34) Chapter 2 is initialed with the letters "A.L.M." and contains 9899 of these letters (19 x 521).

(35) Chapter 3 is also initialed with the letters "A.L.M." and contains 5662 of these letters (19 x 298).

(36) Chapters 29, 30, 31, & 32 are also initialed with the letters "A.L.M." and the total frequency of occurrence of these letters is 1672 (19 x 88), 1254 (19 x 66), 817 (19 x 43), and 570 (19 x 30), respectively.

(37) Chapters 10 and 11 are intialed with the letters "A.L.R.," and contain exactly the same total frequency of occurrence, namely, 2489 each (19 x 131).

(38) Chapters 12, 14, and 15 are also initialed with the three letters "A.L.R." The total frequency of occurrence of these letters in these chapters is 2375 (19 x 125), 1197 (19 x 63), and 912 (19 x 48), respectively.

**Summary & Conclusions** (cont'd):

(39) Chapter 13 is prefixed with the four initials "A.L.M.R." and contains a total of 1482 of these letters (19 x 78).

(40) Chapter 7 is initialed with the four letters "A.L.M.S." and the frequency of occurrence of these four letters in this chapter is 5320, or 19 x 280.

(41) The number of Quranic initials is 14, and the alphabet letters which participate in making these initials are also 14, and the number of initialed chapters is 29. When we add these numbers, 14+14+29, we find the total 57, or 19 x 3.

(42) The Quranic initials are described as "Miracle of the Quran" (see Page 240).

(43) The common denominator throughout Quran is the number [19], and this is the numerical value of the Arabic word "ONE=Waahid." Thus, this miracle emphasizes the theme of Quran and its basic message: **"GOD IS ONE."**

## CONCLUSION:

The physical evidence presented here proves:
(1) The divine source of Quran.
(2) The perfect integrity and preservation of Quran.

## QURAN: ONLY SOURCE OF GUIDANCE  (6: 19)

Accepting any other sources of guidance constitutes the setting up of other gods beside God;  IDOL-WORSHIP.
------------------------------------------------------------

THIS  IMPORTANT  STATEMENT  HAPPENS  TO  BE

No.  ⟨ 19 ⟩  :

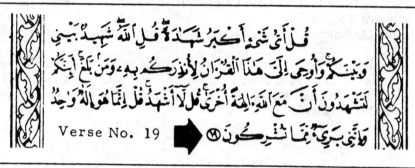

Verse No. 19 ➡️

"Say (O Muhammad), 'Whose testimony is greater?' Say,
'God is my witness that THIS QURAN was given to me to
preach it to you, and whomever it reaches.' Yet, you bear
witness that there are other gods beside God (by upholding
other sources beside Quran).  Say, 'I do not bear such witness.'  Say, 'There is only ONE GOD, and I disown your
idol-worship.'"        ( 6: 19 )
------------------------------------------------------------

This crucial verse happens to be No.  ⟨ 19 ⟩

WE LEFT NOTHING OUT OF THIS BOOK (QURAN)

( 6: 38)

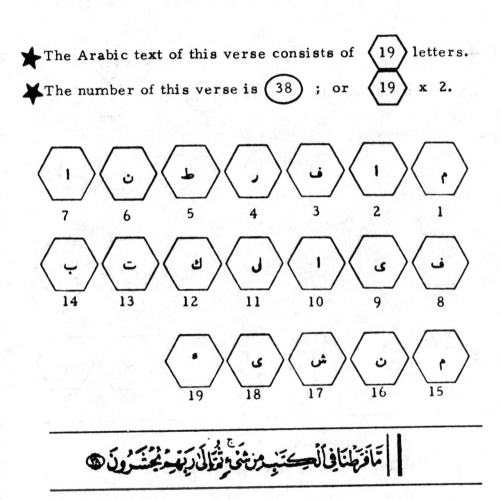

★ The Arabic text of this verse consists of ⟨19⟩ letters.

★ The number of this verse is (38) ; or ⟨19⟩ x 2.

GOD REVEALED THIS BOOK <u>FULLY DETAILED</u>

( 6: 114 )

★ The Arabic text of this verse consists of ⟨19⟩ letters.

★ The number of this verse is (114) ; or ⟨19⟩ x 6.

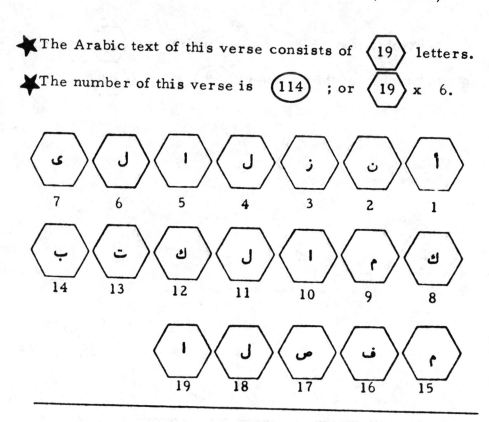

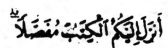

(6: 114)

THE WORD OF YOUR LORD (THIS QURAN) IS
COMPLETE , IN TRUTH AND JUSTICE (6: 115).

This statement consists of ⟨19⟩ letters in the Arabic text.

| | | | | | | |
|---|---|---|---|---|---|---|
| ة | م | ل | ك | ت | م | ت |
| 7 | 6 | 5 | 4 | 3 | 2 | 1 |

| | | | | | | |
|---|---|---|---|---|---|---|
| ا | ق | د | ص | ك | ب | ر |
| 14 | 13 | 12 | 11 | 10 | 9 | 8 |

| | | | | |
|---|---|---|---|---|
| ا | ل | د | ع | و |
| 19 | 18 | 17 | 16 | 15 |

تَمَّتْ كَلِمَتُ رَبِّكَ صِدْقًا وَعَدْلًا

## MUHAMMAD FORBIDDEN FROM ANTICIPATING QURAN

The Prophet Muhammad received an order from God enjoining him from uttering Quranic material without authorization, and ordering him to adhere strictly to Quran and follow it, once it is revealed.

This verse is No. 114, in Chapter 20.

$$114 \quad = \quad \langle 19 \rangle \quad \times \quad 6$$

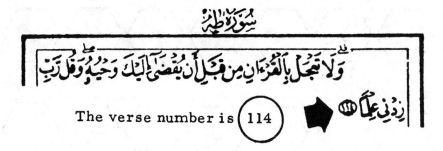

The verse number is 114

Could it be coincidental that the number of this verse is the same as the total number of suras in Quran?

God and His messenger want us to uphold Quran, the whole Quran, and nothing but Quran.

## MUHAMMAD FORBIDDEN FROM EXPLAINING QURAN

There are those who claim that Quran is too difficult to understand, and that "Hadith & Sunna" are needed to explain Quran. First of all, one look at Quran and "Hadith" convinces the reader that the opposite is true. Because the fabricators of "Hadith" belonged to various tribes and even countries, with various dialects, slangs, and accents, the language of "Hadith" is in fact extremely difficult.

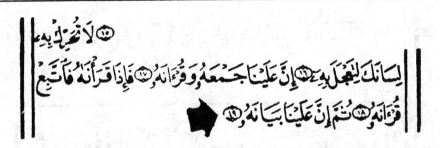

"Do not move your tongue (O Muhammad) to hasten the revelation of Quran. It is we who will put it together as a Quran. Once we reveal it, YOU SHALL FOLLOW IT. Then, it is we who will explain it." ( 75: 16-19 )

The verse stating that God is the one who explains Quran

happens to be verse No. ⟨ 19 ⟩

## QURAN CONTAINS ALL THE EXAMPLES WE NEED

There are four scattered verses stating generally that Quran contains all the examples, allegories, or similitudes that we need. These verses are 17:89, 18:54, 30:58, & 39:27. By adding the verse numbers of these four crucial verses, the total is 228, or 19 x 12.

$$89 + 54 + 58 + 27 = 228 = \boxed{19} \times 12.$$

وَلَقَدْ صَرَّفْنَا لِلنَّاسِ فِي هَذَا الْقُرْآنِ مِن كُلِّ مَثَلٍ فَأَبَىٰ أَكْثَرُ النَّاسِ إِلَّا كُفُورًا ﴿٨٩﴾

وَلَقَدْ صَرَّفْنَا فِي هَٰذَا الْقُرْآنِ لِلنَّاسِ مِن كُلِّ مَثَلٍ ۚ وَكَانَ الْإِنسَانُ أَكْثَرَ شَيْءٍ جَدَلًا ﴿٥٤﴾

وَلَقَدْ ضَرَبْنَا لِلنَّاسِ فِي هَٰذَا الْقُرْآنِ مِن كُلِّ مَثَلٍ ۚ وَلَئِن جِئْتَهُم بِآيَةٍ لَّيَقُولَنَّ الَّذِينَ كَفَرُوا إِنْ أَنتُمْ إِلَّا مُبْطِلُونَ ﴿٥٨﴾ كَذَٰلِكَ يَطْبَعُ اللَّهُ عَلَىٰ قُلُوبِ الَّذِينَ لَا يَعْلَمُونَ

(Continued on the next page)

(Continued from the previous page)

وَلَقَدْ ضَرَبْنَا لِلنَّاسِ فِي هَٰذَا الْقُرْآنِ مِن كُلِّ مَثَلٍ لَّعَلَّهُمْ يَتَذَكَّرُونَ ۝ قُرْآنًا عَرَبِيًّا غَيْرَ ذِي عِوَجٍ لَّعَلَّهُمْ يَتَّقُونَ ۝ ضَرَبَ اللَّهُ مَثَلًا رَّجُلًا فِيهِ شُرَكَآءُ مُتَشَاكِسُونَ وَرَجُلًا سَلَمًا لِّرَجُلٍ هَلْ يَسْتَوِيَانِ مَثَلًا ۚ الْحَمْدُ لِلَّهِ ۚ بَلْ أَكْثَرُهُمْ لَا يَعْلَمُونَ ۝ إِنَّكَ مَيِّتٌ وَإِنَّهُم مَّيِّتُونَ ۝ ثُمَّ إِنَّكُمْ يَوْمَ الْقِيَامَةِ عِندَ رَبِّكُمْ تَخْتَصِمُونَ ۝ فَمَنْ أَظْلَمُ مِمَّن كَذَبَ عَلَى اللَّهِ وَكَذَّبَ بِالصِّدْقِ إِذْ جَآءَهُ ۚ أَلَيْسَ فِي جَهَنَّمَ مَثْوًى لِّلْكَافِرِينَ ۝

The verse numbers of the four verses are 89, 54, 58, and 27.

$$89 + 54 + 58 + 27 = 228$$

$$228 = \langle 19 \rangle \times 12$$

The verses shown above further state that Muhammad is a human being who dies like the rest of us, and that we shall follow  ONE SOURCE of law, rather than a number of contradicting sources.   The  ONE  SOURCE  is identified in verse 28 above as QURAN.

## HADITH: WHERE THEY FIND ANYTHING THEY WISH

Finally, here is a piece of PHYSICAL EVIDENCE informing us that the believers can be distinguished by the fact that
they follow THE ONE CONSISTENT SOURCE (Quran),
while the disbelievers follow "a book wherein they find anything they want." It is well known that we can find anything
we want in the books of "Hadith."

The statement, in the form of a question to the disbelievers,
says, "DO YOU FOLLOW A BOOK WHEREIN YOU FIND
ANYTHING YOU WANT?"

This important statement happens to be No. (38)

38 = 〈19〉 x 2

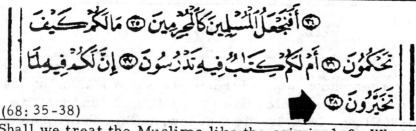

(68: 35-38)

"Shall we treat the Muslims like the criminals? What is
wrong with your judgment? DO YOU FOLLOW A BOOK
WHEREIN YOU FIND ANYTHING YOU WANT?"

GOD CALLS QURAN: **COMPLETE** (6: 115)

GOD CALLS QURAN: **FULLY DETAILED** (6: 114)

GOD CALLS QURAN: **PERFECT** (6: 38)

THE PROPHET DELIVERS QURAN ALONE (69: 40-47)

HADITH & SUNNA ARE BLASPHEMOUS INNOVATIONS (6: 112 & 25: 31)

**YOU SHALL UPHOLD QURAN ALONE** (6: 19; 7: 3; etc.)

GOD PROVIDED **EVEN PHYSICAL EVIDENCE** (see Pages 64-72)

**Why then do they fail to see all this???!!!**

## WHY DO THEY FAIL TO BELIEVE GOD ?

Because their hearts inside are denying what they utter with their mouths. They confess belief due to social and educational circumstances, but their hearts inside are denying:

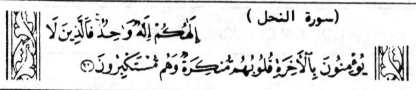

"Your god is ONE GOD. However, those who do not believe in the hereafter, their hearts are denying, and they are too arrogant."          ( 16: 22)

- - - - - - - - - - - - - - - - - - - - - - - - - - - - - - - - - - - - - -

The consequence of this denying (one's deep convictions are denying) is total isolation from Quran:

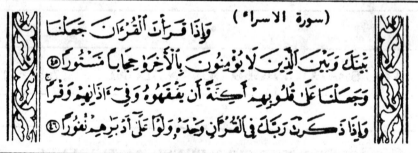

"When you read Quran, we place between you and those who do not believe in the hereafter AN INVISIBLE BARRIER. And we place shields on their hearts to prevent them from understanding it, and deafness in their ears; and when you preach your Lord (ALONE) in the QURAN ALONE they run away in aversion."     (17:45-46)

Therefore, they cannot accept QURAN ALONE ; they look for other sources such as "Hadith & Sunna."

## GUARANTEED VICTORY

The Quran teaches, unequivocally, that victory is
GUARANTEED for the Muslims:

(30: 47) وَكَانَ حَقًّا عَلَيْنَا نَصْرُ ٱلْمُؤْمِنِينَ ۝

" We have decreed that the believers will be victorious. "

إِنَّا لَنَنصُرُ رُسُلَنَا وَٱلَّذِينَ ءَامَنُوا فِى ٱلْحَيَوٰةِ ٱلدُّنْيَا وَيَوْمَ يَقُومُ ٱلْأَشْهَٰدُ ۝

"We will positively grant victory to our messengers, and to
those who believe, both __in this life__ and on the day of resurrection." (40: 51)

وَلَيَنصُرَنَّ ٱللَّهُ مَن يَنصُرُهُ ۗ إِنَّ ٱللَّهَ لَقَوِىٌّ عَزِيزٌ ۝

"God will support with victory those who support Him.  God
is powerful, Almighty."     (22: 40)

إِنَّ ٱللَّهَ يُدَٰفِعُ عَنِ ٱلَّذِينَ ءَامَنُوٓا ۗ إِنَّ ٱللَّهَ لَا يُحِبُّ كُلَّ خَوَّانٍ كَفُورٍ ۝

"God will surely defend those who believe.  God does not
like any betrayer, disbeliever." (22:38)

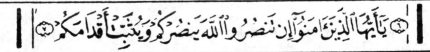

"O you who believe, if you support God, He will grant you
victory, and strengthen your foothold." (47: 7)

# WHY THEN ARE THE MUSLIMS DEFEATED?

In view of the guarantees shown on the previous page, and since God is never wrong, the "Muslims" of today could not possibly be Muslims.

## HISTORICAL FACTS

For as long as the Muslim **Ummah** upheld Quran, and nothing but Quran, the Muslims led the world scientifically, technologically, culturally, socially, militarily, and economically. They never lost a single battle. The borders of Islam extended from West Africa to China; into Southern France and Eastern Germany.

With the appearance of **Hadith & Sunna** at the beginning of the third century AH, a progressive deterioration of the Muslim **Ummah** began. Since the appearance of these innovations as sources of guidance beside the Quran, the "Muslims" never won a single battle.

Why do 3 million Israelis consistently defeat 150 million Arabs???

Does it make any sense that 3 million Israelis should force 1,000 million "Muslims" out of their Mosque in Jerusalem?

Why does India consistently defeat Pakistan? Why do the Russians invade Afghanistan? etc...etc...etc.

## WHY THEN ARE THE "MUSLIMS" DEFEATED?

BECAUSE they refuse to believe God in His repeated statements that Quran is COMPLETE, PERFECT, FULLY DETAILED, and SHALL BE THE ONLY SOURCE OF RELIGIOUS GUIDANCE.

- - - - - - - - - - - - - - - - - - - - - - - - - - - - - - - - - - - - -

Because they have accepted other sources, namely, Hadith and Sunna, beside Quran.

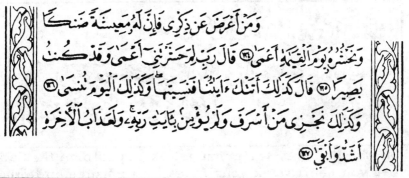

"Whoever disregards My message (Quran) shall have a miserable life, then we will resurrect him, on the Day of Resurrection, blind. He will say, 'My Lord, why did You resurrect me blind, when I used to be a seer (in the first life)?' (God will say), 'This is because Our revelations came to you, but you forgot them, and consequently, today we forget you.' We thus punish those who exceed the limits and refuse to believe the verses of their Lord. And surely, the retribution in the Hereafter is far worse, and everlasting." ( 20: 124-127)

- - - - - - - - - - - - - - - - - - - - - - - - - - - - - - - - - - - - -

## HADITH CAUSED DEVIATION FROM QURAN !

## (1) IS THIS HOW YOU DO YOUR ABLUTION (WUDU)?

Although God's orders are clear and simple in Quran about the observance of ablution, the "Muslim" masses follow another god beside God; they do not do the ablution as prescribed by God. The ultimate result: <u>humiliation & defeat.</u>

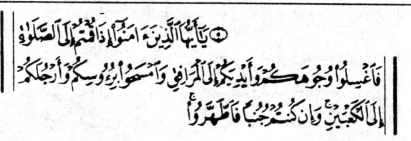

"O you who believe, when you get up to perform the Salat prayers you shall wash your faces, your hands up to the elbows, wipe your heads, and wash your feet." (5: 6)

- - - - - - - - - - - - - - - - - - - - - - - - - - - - - - - - - - - -

The "Muslim" masses today refuse to be satisfied with the commandments of God. They uphold commandments of men, such as the various "imams" and "scholars." As a result, they have a prolonged ablution that depends on which "sect" they follow. All sects resulted from the various "imams" opinions as to how the Prophet is supposed to have done his ablution. Thus, they fell in Satan's trap, disobeyed their Creator, and incurred misery and defeat.

## HADITH CAUSED DEVIATION FROM QURAN !

## (2) IS THIS HOW YOU DO YOUR SALAT PRAYERS?

(17: 110) ۝ وَلَا تَجْهَرْ بِصَلَاتِكَ وَلَا تُخَافِتْ بِهَا وَابْتَغِ بَيْنَ ذَٰلِكَ سَبِيلًا

"When you observe your Salat prayers, your voice shall not be too loud, nor too low; you shall maintain an intermediate tone." ( 17: 110 )

------------------------------------------------

Despite these straightforward instruction from God, the "Muslim" masses were diverted by Hadith; they maintain total silence during the noon prayer, the afternoon prayer, the third unit of the sunset prayer, and the second half of the night prayer. WHERE DID THEY GET THESE INSTRUCTIONS ? From another god beside God; from other sources beside Quran.

------------------------------------------------

Thus, they fell en masse in Satan's traps, and disobeyed their Creator, whose word (Quran) is complete, perfect, and fully detailed (6: 19, 38, & 114).

## HADITH CAUSED DEVIATION FROM QURAN

(3) Do you mention other names beside God's in Salat ?

It is God's commandment that we shall not mention any names in our Salat prayers, beside the name of God (72:18).

------------------------------------------------------------

But the Muslim masses today follow the innovations that dictate upon them the praising and glorifying of Muhammad and Abraham, while praying to their Lord.

وَأَنَّ ٱلْمَسَٰجِدَ لِلَّهِ فَلَا تَدْعُوا۟ مَعَ ٱللَّهِ أَحَدًا ۞

"The mosques belong to God; therefore, do not mention any other names beside the name of God." (72: 18)

------------------------------------------------------------

WHAT IS MORE CLEAR THAN THAT ?

------------------------------------------------------------

The "Muslims" have been duped by Satan into uttering the innovation known as "Tashahhud" where they shower praises and glorifications on Muhammad and Abraham.

------------------------------------------------------------

It should be noted that even the sources of Hadith & Sunna recognize "Tashahhud" as an innovation which is not part of the Salat prayers !

------------------------------------------------------------

IS THIS NOT FLAGRANT IDOL-WORSHIP ???

---

HADITH & SUNNA     vs     GOD'S   LAW

---

After stating that the law against adultery is "perfectly clear," the Quranic commandment orders us to punish the adulterers by whipping them one hundred lashes.

Did the Muslims follow and obey their Creator?   NO.

The Muslim "scholars" declared that the Quranic law is not clear !!! They claimed that the adulterers are not defined in Quran with regard to their marital status, and that they need Hadith to clarify Quran !!!

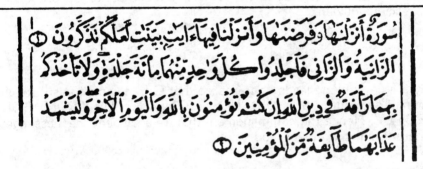

"This Sura we send down, and decree as law, and send down in it verses that are perfectly clear, that you may take heed, The adulteress and adulterer, you shall whip each of them a hundred lashes, and do not be deterred by kindness from carrying our God's law, if you truly believe in God and the Last Day. Let a group of believers witness their punishment."     (24: 1-2)

------------------------------------------------

Overcome by tradition, and Satan's influence, the "Muslim" scholars instituted "stoning to death" as the punishment for married adulterers !!!

## OBEY GOD AND OBEY THE MESSENGER

Satan succeeded in duping millions of Muslims into believing that **obeying God means obeying the Quran, while obeying the messenger means obeying Hadith.**

What helped in popularizing this Satanic trick was the general ignorance of Quran among the Muslim masses, and their failure to heed the divine commandments that Quran shall be the **ONLY SOURCE** of jurisprudence and/or religious guidance.

Only a little thinking leads us to realize that Quran came to us through Muhammad's mouth, and DID NOT COME TO US FROM GOD **DIRECTLY**. Hence the commandment that we shall obey the messenger ...for he utters the words of God.

All previous scriptures have stated the same Quranic truth that: "Whoever obeys the messenger is obeying God." Since the messenger obviously is not God, the commandment clearly means obeying the words of God uttered by the messenger.

The knowledgable and fortunate beli·evers, therefore, realize that Hadith & Sunna are Satanic fabrications aimed at diverting people from the path of God.

# MUHAMMAD'S HADITHS ARE NOT MUHAMMAD'S

Instead, they are the **Hadiths** (narrations) of men and women who never saw the Prophet; in fact, the grandparents of their grandparents never saw the Prophet.

It is well known that the first book of **Hadith** is that of Bukhary, who was born more than 200 years after the death of Muhammad. When Bukhary wrote his book of **Hadiths**, he used to visit the people whom he knew as sources. After verifying that his source is "truthful," and known as a man or woman of righteousness, Bukhary would ask, "Do you know a **Hadith**?" The person would answer, "Yes," then proceed to narrate the "**Hadith**" as follows:
"I heard my father, may God bless his soul, say that he heard his older brother, may God bless his soul, say that he was sitting with his grandmother, may God bless her soul, and she told him that she was having dinner one day with her great uncle, may God bless his soul, when he stated that his maternal grandfather knew Imam Ahmad ibn Muhammad al-Amawy, who mentioned that his grandfather heard from his oldest uncle that he met the great companion of the Prophet Omar ibn Khaled Al-Yamany, and he told him that the Prophet, peace be upon him, said, '.......'"

Thus, the **Hadith** is simply a narration by Bukhary's source, claiming that he or she heard something about the Prophet across eight generations of the dead.

On the other hand, we now possess **irrefutable physical evidence** that Quran is the infallible word of God, and that it was uttered by the Prophet Muhammad. Therefore, we obey the messenger by obeying Quran; nothing but Quran.

# OBEYING HADITH IS NOT OBEYING THE MESSENGER

Instead, it is obedience to the men and women who narrated the "Hadiths."

Obeying the so-called "Hadith of the Prophet," is in fact obeying a group of simple-minded people who thought that the Prophet had said something more than 200 years before they were born.

Thus, if the narrator of a given Hadith is for example a Abbas ibn Yasser, then obeying the Hadith narrated by Abbas ibn Yasser is in fact obeying Abbas ibn Yasser, and has nothing to do with obeying the Prophet.

The true obedience of the Prophet Muhammad is only by obeying Quran, which was indeed uttered by Muhammad, and is supported by indisputable PHYSICAL EVIDENCE.

These facts explain the Quran's repeated statements that "Only those with intelligence take heed."

The Quran was delivered to us through Muhammad's mouth, without any mediators or narrators. The Quran came through Muhammad's mouth, directly to the ears of the revelation writers who scrupulously wrote it down the moment it was uttered.

Thus, Quran is the only true Hadith of Muhammad. Furthermore, the Almighty has guaranteed the eternal preservation of His words, as uttered by Muhammad (15: 9).

# THE GREAT DISASTER

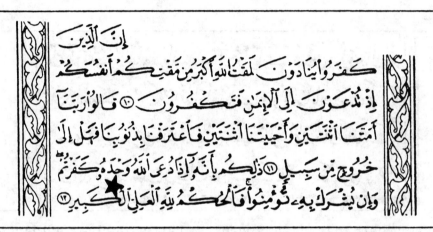

"(On the day of judgment) the disbelievers will be told, 'God's abhorrence towards you is far worse than your own abhorrence towards yourselves, for you were invited to the faith but refused.' They will say, 'Our Lord, You gave us two deaths and two lives, and now we confess our sins; IS THERE ANYWAY OUT?' That is because when GOD ALONE was advocated, you refused to believe. But when idols were advocated along with Him, you believed. Therefore, judgment now belongs with God, the most high, the great." (40: 10-12)

------------------------------------------------------------

When GOD ALONE is advocated, do you believe? OR Do you have to have others advocated along with Him?

------------------------------------------------------------

## THE GREAT DISASTER

فَلَمَّا جَاءَتْهُمْ رُسُلُهُم بِالْبَيِّنَاتِ فَرِحُوا بِمَا عِندَهُم مِّنَ الْعِلْمِ وَحَاقَ بِهِم مَّا كَانُوا بِهِ يَسْتَهْزِءُونَ ۞ فَلَمَّا رَأَوْا بَأْسَنَا قَالُوا آمَنَّا بِاللَّهِ وَحْدَهُ وَكَفَرْنَا بِمَا كُنَّا بِهِ مُشْرِكِينَ ۞ فَلَمْ يَكُ يَنفَعُهُمْ إِيمَانُهُمْ لَمَّا رَأَوْا بَأْسَنَا سُنَّتَ اللَّهِ الَّتِي قَدْ خَلَتْ فِي عِبَادِهِ وَخَسِرَ هُنَالِكَ الْكَافِرُونَ ۞

"When their messengers went to them with clear evidence, they were satisfied with the knowledge they already had, and the very thing they ridiculed caused their doom. Then, when they saw our retribution, they said, 'NOW WE BELIEVE IN GOD ALONE AND WE REJECT OUR PREVIOUS IDOLATRY.' But alas, their belief is useless to them after they see our retribution. Such is God's law which is never changeable; such disbelievers are doomed." (40:83-5)

------------------------------------------------

Are you happy and satisfied with the knowledge you inherited from your parents, elders, or scholars? (Hadith & Sunna)

------------------------------------------------

Are you willing to give up such knowledge, in favor of God's teachings?  OR, will it be too late for you?

------------------------------------------------

## THE    GREAT    CRITERION

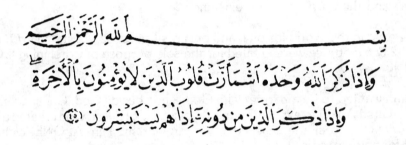

**When God ALONE is advocated, the hearts of those who do not believe in the hereafter shrink with aversion. But when idols are mentioned besides Him, they rejoice (39:45).**

## CLARIFICATION:

## WHY WE ARE HERE?

The whole matter of Quran vs **Hadith & Sunna** becomes clear once we understand the purpose of our existence.

We exist in this world for one, and only one, purpose. As stated in Quran (67: 1-2 & 51: 56) we were created for the sole purpose of worshiping GOD ALONE.

Satan wanted to be a partner with God; a god beside God. Consequently, God created Adam to expose Satan's rebellious ideas. And God created us to show Satan, and all the angels that we can worship Him ALONE, without need for any partners.

- - - - - - - - - - - - - - - - - - - - - - - - - - - - - - - - - - - - - - - - - - - - - - - - - - - -

The purpose of our existence, therefore, is to worship God ALONE. This is why **the only unforgivable offense is idol-worhip.** That is because once we idolize anyone, or anything, beside God, we fail the test.

- - - - - - - - - - - - - - - - - - - - - - - - - - - - - - - - - - - - - - - - - - - - - - - - - - - -

We fulfill the purpose of our existence only if we succeed in worshiping **GOD ALONE, without idolizing Muhammad, or Jesus, or Mary, or any saint, or any imam, or anyone, or anything.**

When we seek "religious" instructions from Muhammad, or any other source beside God, we support Satan in his claim that God needs a partner. Therefore, those who worship God <u>ALONE</u> follow the instructions and teachings of G O D A L O N E. As shown throughout this book, God's teachings are complete, perfect, and fully detailed in Quran.

## FINALLY: MOST IMPORTANT QUESTION

In your mind, can God survive **ALONE**???

Or, does God need Muhammad, in your mind, in order to be commemorated and worshiped???

In your mind, can **GOD ALONE** survive?

Or, does God need a partner, in your mind, such as Muhammad, Jesus, Mary, or some saint(s)???

Would you be perfectly happy and content if you knew about **GOD ALONE**, without Muhammad, Jesus, Mary, or any saint, or anyone, or anything?

Are you annoyed by talking about **GOD ALONE**?

When I keep talking about **GOD ALONE**, does this annoy you? Do you have to hear other names along with God? Can **GOD ALONE** survive in your mind?

When I repeat, and repeat, my talk about **GOD ALONE**, do you feel any repulsion? Or, are you happy and content with the talk about **GOD ALONE**???

Based on the **Great Quranic criterion**, as stated in 39: 45, your answers to these questions provide the key to knowing yourself, and your destiny.

# Related Books by Rashad Khalifa

## THE COMPUTER SPEAKS
Computer analysis of the Quran's text. Detailed data are presented in tables. Illustrations, and full explanations. The book was made possible by the consistent mathematical pattern discovered throughout the Quran.
250 pages, paperback, ISBN 0-934894-38-8

## QURAN: VISUAL PRESENTATION OF THE MIRACLE
The extensive data presented in the above book is superimposed on the Quran's Arabic text. Thus, the intricate mathematical system can be visually noted and appreciated.
250 pages, paperback, ISBN 0-934894-30-2

## QURAN: THE FINAL TESTATMENT (English Only) - Revised Edition III
Translated From the Original. Comprehensive Index, Footnotes, Appendices
570 pages, library edition, Durable Cover, ISBN 1-881893-05-7

## QURAN: THE FINAL TESTAMENT (with Arabic Text) - Revised Edition II
Translated From the Original. Comprehensive Index, Footnotes, Appendices
800 pages, library edition, English with Arabic text, ISBN 1-881893-03-0

## QURAN, HADITH AND ISLAM
A comprehensive study of the role of *Hadith* in corrupting today's Islam. The Quran's mathematical code is applied as a criterion to expose *Hadith* and *Sunna* as satanic innovations which have nothing to do with the Prophet Mohammad.
96 pages, paperback, ISBN 0-934894-35-3

# Other Books

## JESUS: MYTHS AND MESSAGE
Development of Christian doctrine by Lisa Spray
250 pages, paperback, ISBN 1-881893-00-6

## HADITH: A RE-EVALUATION
The role of Hadith in Islam by Kassim Ahmad
300 pages, paperback, ISBN 1-881893-02-0

## BEYOND PROBABILITY
God's Message in Mathematics by Abdullah Arik
Paperback

# Newsletter

## THE TIMES OF UNIVERSAL UNITY
Quarterly news bulletin of Universal Unity

## SUBMITTERS PERSPECTIVE
Monthly news bulletin of International Community of Submitters/Masjid Tucson.
ISSN 1089-53X

Many more. Other Islamic publications are available. Ask for a free catalog.

Universal Unity
1860 Mowry Ave. Suite 400
Fremont, CA 94538 USA
Fax: (510)794-9783
Web site: http://www.universalunity.net
e-mail: books@universalunity.net

United Submitters International
Masjid tucson
PO Box 43476
Tucson, AZ 85733-3476
Tel/Fax (520)323-7636
Web site: http://www.masjidtucson.org
Web site: http://www.submission.org